SAINT FRANCIS

THE HERALD OF THE GREAT KING

D1009022

A SKETCH BY
NESTA DE ROBECK

CASA EDITRICE FRANCESCANA
FRATI MINORI CONVENTUALI
Italy - 06082 ASSISI

TO
FATHER AND MOTHER

PREFACE

It takes a saint, a writer of imaginative genius, and a great scholar to write about Saint Francis: and yet there is a certain excuse for the rest of us whose only claim is that of loving him.

Saint Francis is inexhaustible; he turns his back on no one; to each he shows something of himself, and enriches all who approach him.

The material concerning his life is very extensive, and the few episodes of this booklet are a bare minimum taken from the many that are recounted in the early records.

Here there is nothing original: I have merely picked up a few crumbs from the table of all the modern writers on Saint Francis, especially Fr: Cuthbert, Sabatier, Joergensen, Fortini and Karrer, and I am also deeply indebted to the numerous scholars belonging to the Franciscan Order whose researches and conclusions have appeared in various Franciscan periodicals.

I have taken my quotations from the Two Legends by Thomas of Celano Saint Francis' first official biographer, from the legend by Saint Bonaventure, the Mirror of Perfection and the Fioretti; and have used used the Latin Italian and English versions.

My particular thanks are due to Father Giuseppe Zaccaria O.F.M. Conv.: without whose help this sketch would never have been written.

ASSISI - Anno Santo 1975

NESTA DE ROBECK

ASSISI is almost to the centre of Italy: Dante, playing on the name called it «the Orient» because in it «there was born to the world a sun». This sun is Saint Francis, and the light which emanates from him has illuminated and warmed each generation for seven hundred years. He is always present: behind us historically; beside us as a living friend and guide; he beckons to us from another world; and we seem to hear his own words: «I want to send you all to Heaven».

In Assisi his life story is extraordinarily vivid: so much has remained unchanged, and as we look at buildings he knew, and walk along paths he must have trodden, we almost expect to meet him round the next corner. He was familiar with all the moods of sunrise and sunset from Assisi, as with the luminous tenderness of the lines and colour of the wide southern view over the valley of Spoleto; he knew all the grandeur and rugged strength of the contrasting northern view from the castle hill. Indeed this accentuated contrast between north and south in the landscape of Assisi is reflected in the character of its people; we find it in Francis himself.

Beyond all this however Francis has left something else of himself for those who come in search of him. Multitudes have felt, and feel the pervading sense of peace, and this was what he wished in the last blessing given to Assisi, and which he prayed might endure.

ASSISI - Panorama

BEFORE 1182 · THE HISTORY OF ASSISI

The Assisi of Francis was like many another of the small,
ancient cities of Italy. It had lain just beyond the border of
the Etruscan kingdom, and became a vassal of Rome in
300 B.C. The Romans built a beautiful city with green ter-
races facing southwards, with forum, theatre, amphi-

The bigger Fortress

theatre and many temples as well as agreeable villas. The poet Propertius was born here.

In the third century A.D. Christianity was preached by Saint Felicianus, Saint Vittorinus, and Saint Rufinus who became the city's patron saint. These three with many of their followers were martyred. There is a direct link between this period of the martyrs and Franciscan history in the chapel of Saint Mary of the Angels, known as the Porziuncula, and which is said to have been built by some pilgrims returning from the Holy Land in the fourth century. It was one of Assisi's most ancient Christian sanctuaries; dedicated to Our Lady, and legend says that there angels could often be heard singing her praises.

Assisi came in for its share of fighting during the waves of invasions which swept into and over Italy with almost tidal regularity, and naturally each one left its mark.

While the Huns overan northern Italy, Rome was sacked by Alaric and his Visigoths, and Theodoric the greatest of the Ostrogoths ruled in Ravenna. In the sixth century Totila took and sacked Assisi; then the Goths were succeeded by the Longobards and the Assisan chronicles describe them as being «exceedingly fierce and terrible». Italy was divided into new principalities and Assisi was included in the duchy of Spoleto. In the eighth century history took a new turn and the Franks arrived; Assisi was besieged, sacked, an the inhabitants massacred; then rebuilding began, apparently by Charlemagne's order.

The duchy of Spoleto passed under Frankish control, and there must have been a period of at least relative peace and prosperity. The general panic over the year 1000 seems to have coincided with a new wave of veneration for the city's martyrs which may have been partly the result of everyone's relief that the end of the world had not happened! It was the people of Assisi who wished that a grand new church should be built in Saint Rufino's honour; a century later this first church, which also became the cathedral, seemed inadequate to a generation that was being rapidly enriched through expanding commerce, and Giovanni di Gubbio was commissioned to rebuild it. His façade, which is still one of Assisi's glories, was seen by Francis.

Violence and corruption, spiritual illumination and achievement went side by side through the eleventh and twelfth centuries. It was the moment of the Crusades, and of the first flowering of national cultures within the framework of a united European Christian civilisation; each generation handed on a wonderfully increasing inheritance, in the small cities and much as in the great. Every-

The stable where St. Francis was born

where genius was at work with every art and craft; the great tales of chivalry were being told, the Arthurian cycle of legends was just emerging, poets too had started singing in the vernacular, and every castle was the haunt of troubadours, and minstrels.

The unity of Christendom proclaimed by the scholars and artists of the Middle Ages was roughly that of every man, and it shone in the lives of many saints. Great orders were coming into being following in the steps of Saint Benedict: there were for example the Camaldolese founded by Saint Romuald, the Carthusians by Saint Bruno, the Vallombrosians by Saint Giovanni Gualberto, the Premonstratensians by Saint Norbert. Everywhere scholars «were fighting the devil by pen and ink»; and there were such powerful visionaries as Saint Hildegarden, Saint Michtilde, Saint Elisabeth of Schoenau and Saint Gertrude. The spirtual life was not theoretical; it was being lived through strong and dynamic personalities.

But there was another side to the picture: one of wars, divisions, corruption and violence. Italy was rent by continual invasions, each bringing untold suffering: yet the spiritual forces asserted themselves and genius still speaks to us in the wonderful buildings and treasures of art of the so-called dark ages. Alongside of heretical sects there were men and women who felt the attraction of the evangelical life and remained within the Church living under a rule of voluntary poverty and chastity. These Poor Men of Lyons and Umiliati as they were called were pointing to the future: they and the whole world were waiting for Francis.

Political upheavals in Rome, and the violent efforts of would-be reformers brought another invasion of Italy, this time by red-haired Frederick of Hohenstaufen. This romantic adventurer dreamed of himself as the heir of Constantine and Charlemagne; and his descent into Italy in 1154 started a long swaying struggle full of conflicting loyalties, interest and sympathies, and in which the rival claims of Papacy and Empire were set for a duel; Guelph and Ghibelline had become realities.

At one moment Spoleto was burned as a result of rebellion, and Barbarossa warned Assisi that he considered the city as imperial territory. He was able to raze the walls of Milan and to carry off the bodies of the Three Kings to Cologne; but in their turn the independent-spirited northern Italian Communes defeated him at Legnano. Through the marriage of his son Henry to the heiress of Sicily, central Italy found itself sandwiched between imperial forces coming in from the north and their stronghold in the south. The individual city states were increasingly threatened.

In 1174 Assisi had been subdued by Frederick's troops, and three years later he came in person and established himself in the newly enlarged and fortified castle known as the Rocca. His kinsman Conrad of Luetzen was made Duke of Spoleto, and ruled Assisi as an imperial fief; ruled it apparently with a light hand, but even so the people were restive, and everywhere citizens were increasing in wealth and power and determination to be independent. Thus the stage in Assisi was set for the coming of Francis.

THE CHILDHOOD OF ST. FRANCIS
(1182-1202)

Pietro Bernardone of the Moriconi family was a hardworking and successful cloth merchant and with others of his kind frequented the great European fairs in which fortunes could be made and useful contacts established. It was during one of his absences that his wife Pica who is said to have been of Provençal origin gave birth to their eldest son. Later legends say that Francis was born in a stable, and that during his baptism in the Cathedral font which is still in use, a venerable old man took the child in his arms predicting a great future for him. He was christened with the name of Giovanni; but Pietro insisted that he should be called Francesco, Francis, the Frenchman: the only pet name to enter the Litany of the Saints. Francis was the child of his very vital age. The world was opening out and new opportunities were coming into view. Those children spoke a mixture of Latin and Umbrian-Italian; and Francis also had some French for we hear of him singing French songs. Danger and adventure were always in the air and the ferocious Saracen mercenaries of the Emperor appeared all too often to harry the valley of Spoleto.

The Assisi little Francis knew was the typical mediaeval city enclosed within its walls, yet in close touch with the countryside, its artists and artisans kept busy by the city's self-sufficient life. Besides the feudal nobility, the citzens were roughly divided into two classes, the Majores and Minores, and by birth Francis belonged to the Majores. For the children, the year was punctuated by the colourful festivals of the Church and the Commune; they certainly joined in the Calendimaggio revels which ushered in the month of May, and played in the streets as the boys do to-day. A number of buildings, churches, castles, gates and streets have remained much as they were when Francis was alive.

The streets provided varied entertainment with fairs and strolling players, broils and processions, and Francis may have heard that wandering preacher of whom the Three Companions speak, and who greeted people with the words «Pax et Bonum». He may have been a disciple of the famous Calabrian hermit and prophet Joachim of Flores, who predicted terrible disasters preceding a new epoch of peace, the reign of the Holy Spirit. Many folk were impressed and terrified by Joachim's apocalyptic visions; and he insisted that the only remedy for the world's ills was the mending of life, and individual sanctity. Thirty years later that greeting «Pax et Bonum» would be repeated all over Europe by all kinds of people because the spark of love in the heart of one small Assisan boy had been kindled by the Holy Spirit into an overwhelming flame of love of God and men.

The child became a big boy, a ringleader in every prank, the pride of his father's heart, and Pietro grudged no

Francis gives away his cloak

money to his extravagant son who liked to dress as a prince, and be acclaimed as the king of every revel. Yet he was always known for his courtesy to everyone: and it was perhaps from this natural disposition that there grew his later attitude described by Chesterton when he said that Francis «was a courtier in a world of kings».

He had been to the school of the church of San Giorgio, and Pietro naturally wished that his talents should turn into improving the family business and status. One of the first sights we catch of Francis is in his father's shop when a beggar asked for money: it was an inopportune moment and the alms were refused. But the beggar had not gone far before Francis, filled with rumors, caught up to him, vowing that he would never refuse a request made in the name of God.

When Francis was twelve, two other children were born, also in Assisi, the son of the Emperor Henry VI, who was baptized Frederick and Chiara, Clare, the daughter of a powerful Assisan noble Favarone. Francis may have actually seen those babies being carried to the cathedral; certainly no one then could have dreamed that the names of those three children would have universal fame.

In 1197 the Emperor Henry died, and the following year Innocent III became Pope. By this time Barbarossa was a legend, and Innocent was bent on subjecting the imperial power, and in turning the foreigner out of Italy. He demanded that the duchy of Spoleto should be handed over to the Holy See, Conrad of Luetzen fled, and the citizens of Assisi enthusiastically started to demolish the castle. It was a rising of the native population against the foreigner, of the Guelph against the Ghibelline, and also of the Commune against the Castle. Civil discord raged, and the feudal nobles of Assisi, including Clare's father turned for help to Ghibelline Perugia, Assisi's traditional enemy. A local dispute flared up into a war and Francis marched out with the citizen army of Assisi.

A battle was fought at Ponte San Giovanni; the Perugians were victorious, and Francis was made prisoner with other Assisans. In prison his good humour lightened the

Francis' dream

atmosphere for everyone; it was noticed that he was especially attentive to a very morose fellow captive, and when asked the reason for his consistent gaiety he replied: «because I see the day when the whole world will do me homage». Someone remembered the fantastic boast: thirty years later it had come true.

GOD'S POOR
(1202-1207)

After about a year peace was patched up between Perugia and Assisi, and also between the rival classes of the Majores and Minores. The exiled nobles returned to their homes together with the Assisan prisoners. Francis fell ill, and during those weeks of sickness the first intimations of a different kind of life seem to have crossed his mind. As soon as he was convalescent he crawled out into the sun and leaning on a stick, stood, looking at the view. For the first time that view which he loved failed him: «the beauty of the fields, the delight of the vineyards and all that is fair to the eye, could in no way gladden him whereupon he was amazed at the change which had come upon him so suddenly, and thought them most foolish who could love these things».

However with the return of health and strength Francis' thoughts turned again to fighting, for the struggle between the Papacy and the Empire was still raging. He joined a band of young Assisans who were recruited to go south and link up with the Papal forces under Walter of Brienne. Pietro spared no money in providing him with a sumptuous kit, and no doubt looked forward to seeing Francis win his spurs; what did he think when Francis gave away this outfit to a poor and very shabby knight?

Before leaving Assisi Francis dreamed of a beautiful palace filled with shining suits of silver armour and a beautiful bride, and was told that all this would be for him and his followers. He set out in high spirits declaring «I know I shall become a great prince».

Francis before the Crucifix of San Damian

At Spoleto that dream of promise was followed by another, and he heard a voice asking: «Francis, whom is it better to serve, the lord or the servant?».

«Surely it is better to serve the lord».

«Why then dost thou make a lord of the servant?».

Unhesitatingly Francis replied: «Lord what dost Thou wish me to do?».

He was bidden to return home and he would then learn more.

That return must have been very hard for a young man dreaming of a career of knightly chivalry; it made him appear as rather an ignominious windbag. He took up his old life again as king of the revels but a new note had crept in. His zest for spending was as great as ever, but it too had found fresh channels. Nothing was too beautiful or costly for the service of God, and he was continually sending gifts to poor churches; moreover every beggar seemed to fascinate him: gradually he felt himself a stranger among his former friends. One day he was particularly absentminded during some feast or lark, and his companions twitted him, «why Francis you're in love». The answer came with unexpected, serious conviction: «Yes, I am thinking of taking a bride more noble and beautiful and nicer than any you have ever seen». Perhaps he hardly realized what he was saying; without knowing it, he had turned a corner.

He spent hours wandering about the country, and praying in an ancient forsaken tomb. Sometimes a friend went with him, and he heard Francis crying out in anguish; this friend has sometimes been identified with the future Brother Elias. He was tormented with terrifying fears and visions, but the central experience of those months was a vision of Christ crucified, and Saint Bonaventure tells us that, «Francis' whole soul seemed to melt away: and so deeply was the memory of Christ's passion impressed on his heart, that it pierced even to the marrow of his bone. From that hour whenever he thought of the Passion of Christ he could scarcely retain his tears and sighs».

Francis was still in a state of uncertainty about his future;

Francis honored

and he went off to Rome on a pilgrimage to pray that his way might become clear. In doing so he was following the Catholic custom of his time, since to pray at the tombs of the Apostles ranked next to a pilgrimage to the Holy Places. It was also an early sign of his life-long attachment to Rome, to the Holy See as the heart of the Church. A beggar was standing outside Saint Peter's; perhaps almost before he knew what he was doing, Francis had changed clothes with him, and taken his place. He stayed there till evening, learning what it felt like to beg.

Pietro Bernardone was away when Francis reached home; he asked his mother to prepare a feast, and when she enquired who were to be the guests, Francis replied, «God's poor».

By this time everyone must have noticed that Pietro's son was greatly changed, and no doubt there was plenty of comment, and Pica may have been asked indiscreet questions. She had an answer ready: «I will tell you what this son of mine will become; he will become a son of God».

Again unexpectedly there came another decisive moment when one day Francis came face to face with a leper who begged for charity. He had a horror of leprosy, and it would have been easy to fling this poor man a coin, and pass on. But something rose in Francis compelling him to the hard, to the impossible gesture: he took the lepers hand and kissed it, and then gave him the kiss of peace on his cheek. From that moment Francis became the friend and helper of all lepers. Much later in his Testament he described this change of heart: «The Lord gave to me Brother Francis thus to begin to do penance: for when I was in sin it seemed to me too bitter a thing to see lepers, and the Lord Himself led me amongst them, and I dealt mercifully with them. And when I left them, what had seemed bitter to me, was changed into sweetness of soul and body».

That meeting was a milestone in Francis' life; he was soon to reach another. On the hill below Assisi, near to the place where the martyr Saint Felicianus had first preached Christianity, there was a half ruined chapel dedi-

Francis' renunciation

cated to Saint Damian. Francis went in and knelt before a painted crucifix: it is still preserved by the nuns of Santa Chiara, and on it Christ is portrayed as the king ruling from the cross with no trace of suffering on the calm and gentle face. There is a prayer attributed to Francis which runs: «Great and glorious God, and Thou my Lord Jesus Christ, I pray Thee illuminate the darkness of my heart, and give me pure faith, firm hope and perfect charity, that I may know Thee, and in all act according to Thy holy Will». He may have used some such words that day, and then he heard from the crucifix the clear, calm order, «Francis go and repair my church, which, as thou seest is a ruin». For Francis hesitation was impossible; Christ Himself had spoken. His first action was to offer the priest in charge of the chapel money to keep a lamp burning in front of the Crucifix; then to set about repairing the building. He was still living at home, and because he needed money to procure the necessary materials, he took some of his fathers stuffs, and rode off to Foligno where he sold both the horse and stuffs. He took the money straight to the priest of Saint Damian's who however was so loath to accept it that Francis flung it into his house by a window: after which he managed to persuade the priest to allow him to remain there.

Pietro Bernardone had again been absent; but when he returned and found what had happened he was hotly indignant, and set off with some friends to bring Francis home. Evidently Francis had been warned, and dreading the interview with his father, he fled. But the load of uncertainty had lifted from his mind: he knew what he must do: he had reached the point where obstacles were only relative. He must have realized however that sooner or later he would have to meet his father. Shabby and unkempt he went through the streets begging for bulding materials, pursued by derisive hoots and handfuls of mud. Yet at least one person realized something of the truth, for a simpleton flung his cloak on the ground for Francis to walk over, and this was the first sign of the world's homage to him who was to choose poverty as a privilege.

Marriage with Lady Poverty (Giotto)

One day Pietro Bernardone was in his shop when he heard a tumult in the street. A crowd was coming along, shouting and jeering, and then he saw who was the centre of it all. His son, his Francis to have come to this! To be trailing the family name in the dust! Pietro flung the crowd apart, collared Francis, dragged him back into the house, and locked him into the cellar. It was only when Pietro was next absent from home that Pica liberated Francis, and he went straight back to San Damiano.

Furious, despairing and humiliated Pietro again sought out his son, but Francis was adamant in his decision not to return home, and to take no further orders from his father. Pietro could only fall back on a legal expulsion of his son from the city; but since he could not obtain this from the civil authorities, he sued him in the ecclesiastical court for the return of his stolen property.

There must have been a crowd in the court that day, for Pietro was a «rei publicae benefactor», and everyone knew how he had indulged his son. Francis answered the demand for restitution of the horse and cloth by stripping off his clothes and laying them at his fathers feet with the words: «I will return not only the money which belongs to him, but also the clothes I wear which are his. All of you hear and understand; hitherto I have called Pietro Bernardone my father... now I will say Our Father Who art in Heaven and not father Pietro Bernardone».

Pietro gathered up the clothes and money and turned away «with fury and exceeding sorrow... for he greatly loved him». There is no further mention of the Bernardone family in any Franciscan chronicle, except of Francis' younger brother Angelo. Pietro's trouble was that he could not keep up with the pace of a saint; there is no hint of any later reconciliation between Francis and his parents, but that is not proof that it never happened.

When Francis discarded his clothes, the Bishop wrapped him in his own cloak; and he finally left the court, dressed in a workman's tunic with a length of rope as a belt. He would not have changed these garments for the richest

St. Damiano Shrine

clothes in Christendom, for they were the outward pledge of his marriage to Lady Poverty, a love match if ever there was one. Christ had chosen Poverty; she had been faithful to Him all through His earthly life, she was with Him on the cross and in the sepulchre, closer to Him than anything and anyone; and therefore to Francis she was a beautiful and desirable and beloved lady, and he would be her knight.

ST. FRANCIS RESTORES SAN DAMIANO
(1207-1210)

Thus in his own words Francis «left the world»; he was penniless and immensely exhilarated, and soon started over the hills towards Gubbio singing French songs. He met some robbers who asked who he was. «I am the Herald of the Great King of Heaven», he replied gaily, and had we been with those robbers we should probably have joined in their mirth. Herald indeed! They knew the livery of a herald: this was just a madman, and the bullies set on Francis, beat him, and threw him into the ditch with a «lie there thou fool herald». And he had considerable difficulty in replacing his stolen clothes.

He returned to San Damiano to continue the work of restoration; and whenever he appeared in Assisi, he was pelted with mud and jeers, and if he met his father, with curses. The sting of those curses was bitter, and Francis met them by asking the nearest beggar to bless him in his fathers place. In earlier days he had played the beggar; now he was one, and learnt to know what it meant to ask for scraps of food and to eat whatever he was given. The first time he nearly turned away from the disgusting mess; then he remembered that he was a knight, and that his lady was Poverty. He also had to beg for stones for his work. He would call to passers-by «Come and help in this work, for this very church of Saint Damian's will one day be a convent of ladies whose life and fame will glorify our heavenly Father in all the world».

At the moment it seemed as though Francis' horizon would be bounded by praying, begging, building, and the service of the lepers in a neigbouring leper settlement. It is told that one of these lepers, meeting Francis on the road wished to kiss his footprints but tried to avoid touching him. The leper's face was pitifully ravaged by the disease, but Francis took him in his arms, and kissed him on the mouth, whereat all trace of leprosy disappeared.

When the work at Saint Damian's was finished, Francis continued to restore other churches, among them San

Pietro, Santa Maria Maggiore and Santa Maria degli Angeli, commonly known as the Porziuncola. As usual the Passion of Christ was the centre of his thoughts, and sometimes he would burst into loud lamentations. A passer by asked the cause of such grief: «I am weeping over the Passion of my Lord Jesus Christ, and I will not be ashamed to weep over it to the end of time». The stranger stopped, and he and Francis wept and prayed together.

Francis was nearing another milestone in his life, and he reached it on February 24th the feast of Saint Matthias when the priest read the Gospel during Mass. «Going forth preach, saying: The kingdom of God is at hand... Possess not gold or silver or money in your purses, or scrip for your journey or two coats, or shoes, or a staff.

And when you come into a house salute it saying, "Peace be to this house"». He heard every word of that Gospel as being spoken to him personally: «This is what I have been seeking, this is what my heart yearns for», he exclaimed after Mass to the priest; henceforth he greeted all he met with the words, «Good people, the Lord give you peace». Among the Assisans who had been watching Francis was Bernard of Quintavalle, a rich and respected citizen of noble family. At first he went secretly to see him then invited him to his own house and Francis went with pleasure.

Bernard had had Francis' bed made up in his own room, and was able to see how Francis pretended to sleep, and really spent the night in prayer. Thus he formed the opinion. «Truly this man comes from God». At last he broke the ice with the question, «What should a man do for the best if, having held the property of his Lord for many years, he no longer wishes to retain it?». Naturally Francis replied that the property should be returned. «Then» Bernard went on, «I wish for the love of God and of my Lord Jesus Christ to dispose of all my temporal goods given me by the Lord as may seem best to thee». Another person, Peter Cattaneo, a doctor of Law and a canon of the cathedral was moved to a like decision, and together the three went to the church of Saint Nicholas.

Francis knelt before the altar, praying that God would show them His will, then he opened the Gospels and his eyes fell on the passage from Saint Matthew «If thou would'st be perfected, go sell all that thou hast and give to the poor, and thou shalt have treasure in Heaven; and come and follow Me». Again he opened the book and read the text from Saint Luke: «Take nothing for your journey, neither staff nor scrip, nor bread nor money, neither have two coats». The third time his eyes fell on Saint Matthew's words: «If any man will come after Me, let him deny himself and take up his cross and follow Me».

«Brothers», exclaimed Francis, «this is our life and rule and for all who will join our company».

We can imagine the stir in Assisi when Bernard and Peter publicly gave away their possesions. A priest, Sylvester was standing by, and complained that he had not been sufficiently paid for some stones he had sold to Francis. Money was poured into his hands; and it was not long before Sylvester was desperately ashamed of what he had done. He was the third companion. The next recruit was Giles, a peasant who threw himself on the ground before Francis: «Brother Francis, I want to be with you for the love of God». Unconsciously he was speaking for thousands. Francis turned to him: «Knowest thou how great a favour the Lord has given thee? If my brother the emperor came to Assisi and wished to choose some one to be his knight or chamberlain, how many would claim the honour! How much more highly thou should'st esteem the privilege of being chosen out of many for the court of the Lord». That same day Giles was able to give away his cloak to a beggar woman.

Francis' first idea was that he and his followers should work for their living how and where they could, that they should eat what they were given in return for their services, and when they had nothing that they should beg, that they should sleep anywhere when they were not together.

The service of the lepers was still in the foreground of their days; but they also began to go about the country to

Vision of the fiery chariot

tell anyone who would listen of the peace and joy to be found in following the literal words of the Gospel. When people asked who they were they would answer: «We are men of Assisi who lead a life of penance», but yet these beggars were gay, and one chronicler described them: «They were able to rejoice so much because they had abandoned so much». They came to be known as the «Joculatores Domini». When Francis was speaking Giles would go round among the listeners and say, «Listen to him; what he says is true».

These journeys brought in more followers, Angelo Tancredi, a knight of Rieti, Ruffino, Masseo, Sabbatino, Juniper, Pacifico, Philip, Leo and John, and others followed in quick succession. No men could have been more different from each other, and Francis welcomed all, and all loved him; and at any rate in the early days got on together. There was room for Bernard the contemplative, for Elias the competent, for Juniper the eccentric. Francis once described the perfect Friar Minor as one who «must be as true to Poverty as Bernard, as simple and pure as Leo, as chaste as Angelo, as intelligent and eloquent as Masseo; his mind must be fixed on high like Giles, his prayer must be that of Ruffino whose mind is always with God whether he sleeps or wakes, he must be patient like Juniper, strong in soul and body as John, loving as Roger, and like Lucidus he must never feel settled in one place». Francis sent his brothers out by twos and threes saying: «Go my beloved and announce the Gospel of peace and conversion. Be patient in trouble, give an humble answer to all who insult you, bless them that persecute you... endure all things patiently». The material side of their programme was summed up in the words: «Cast thy care upon the Lord, and He shall sustain thee». Whenever they passed a church they were to bow themselves to the dust and say: «We adore Thee O Christ here and in all Thy churches; and we bless Thee because Thou hast redeemed us by Thy holy cross».

At this time Francis seems to have oscillated spiritually between a tremendous realisation of his own mission;

The Pope's dream

and an equal sense of his own complete insufficiency. With many tears he bewailed his sins, «Lord be merciful to me a sinner». He was in such a mood one time in the mountains above Rieti, and then perhaps some vision gave him the assurance that all his past sins were forgiven, and that he would not fail in his task. He communicated his new certainty to his companions: «My beloved be comforted and rejoice in the Lord, and do not be sad because you seem to be few. Neither let my or your simple ways frighten you; for the Lord has shown me that He will make us increase into a great multitude, and spread abroad to the ends of the earth... I have seen a multitude of men who come desiring to put on the habit of our holy vocation and to live under the rule of our blessed religion; and their sound is in my ears as they come and go under the orders of holy obedience. I have seen the roads from all countries full of men coming here; the French are coming, the Spaniards are hastening, the Germans and English run, and great is the crowd of others who hurry along speaking different tongues... My beloved, in these first days of our dwelling together, it is like eating apples all sweet and pleasant to the taste; a little later the apples offered us will not all be so sweet and pleasant, and in the end some will be so bitter that we shall be unable to eat them though outwardly they will look fair and juicy».

Francis and his first companions were still eating the sweet apples of their own uncontaminated enthusiasm; and their dramatic appeal to the Gospel had the success of novelty; those whose heart and imagination were touched were stirred to reverence, the cynical were tolerant, no doubt prophesying that the movement would certainly die. When however several Assisans had left their families and homes there was also widespread criticism; and as Francis went through the streets to beg he was followed by abuse for throwing perfectly good citizens homeless and penniless on the world.

Bishop Guido who was his firm friend had to take this criticism into account; and he sent for Francis to put the difficulties and dangers of the situation before him. What if

Approval of the Rule by Pope Innocent III

Church of Rivo Torto

people refused to give them alms? Were they to starve? How could a number of men live without a home?

Francis did not hesitate: «My Lord if we keep property we shall need arms to defend ourselves, and we shall be constantly involved in litigation and feuds; and this will often prevent us from loving God and our neighbour. Therefore we desire to possess no temporal goods in this world». The argument was unanswerable: Francis had taken his stand, from which he never moved.

When the Brothers numbered twelve the time seemed to have come when they should ask the Pope's blessing on their way of life. Francis first tried to accost the Pope without any introduction, but was unsuccessful. Bishop Guido was in Rome and no doubt took the matter in hand;

and it is told how that night Innocent dreamed that the disreputable beggar from whom he had turned aside, was supporting the tottering Lateran on his shoulder. Francis and his companions were summoned to an audience.

The two personalities facing each other that day were well matched, for besides being a great statesman, Innocent was an ardent reformer, and his writings are full of a burning piety. He had approved the rule of the Umiliati in spite of the objections of some of his Curia: better than anyone he knew the spiritual crosscurrents of the time and the urgent need of reform. As he listened to Francis' programme he must have asked himself whether this man were not indeed a heaven-sent reformer; but to the majority of the Papal court such a way of life as that the Brothers proposed to lead, appeared to be beyond any possibility of human endurance. Then the Cardinal John of Saint Paul rose, and his argument had something of Francis' commonsense: «If we reject the petition of this poor man, as being new and too hard to fulfill when all he asks is that the law of the Gospel be confirmed to him, let us beware that we do not offend the Gospel of Christ. For if anyone says that in the observance of evangelical perfection, and in the vow to observe it, there is anything new or irrational, or impossible of fulfillment, such a person is convicted of blasphemy against Christ the Author of the Gospel».

Told to speak Francis burst into an impassioned parable of the King's bride who dwelt in the desert, and when her sons sought out their father He recognized them from their likeness to Himself. «Holy Father». he ended, «I am that poor woman whom God so loved, and in His mercy has so honoured».

Innocent dismissed them with the words: «Go forth my brother, and as the Lord shall deign to inspire you, preach repentance to all men. When almighty God has multiplied you in numbers and grace, come to me again rejoicing, and I will grant you more than this, and with greater assurance commit to you further powers». He turned to the

Sheds at Rivo Torto

cardinals: «Truly this is the pious and holy man by whom the Church of God shall be restored».

ST. FRANCIS AND ST. CLARE
(1210-1212)

The brothers left Rome exulting, and in this mood they lingered for a few weeks in the valley of the Nera, so happy that they were tempted to remain there as hermits. But the spirit of the primitive rule drove them on for their duty lay in being missionaries for Christ among their fellow

Porziuncula

men. That primitive rule was extremely simple, and though the text of it was lost, a great deal was incorporated in Francis' own later version. It consisted largely of passages from the Gospel with poverty as the keynote; but Poverty loved as a lady, not suffered as a penance. «O who would not love Lady Poverty above all things; of Thee O Jesus I ask to be signed with this privilege, I long to be enriched with this treasure, I beseech of Thee O most poor Jesus that for Thy sake it may always be the mark of me and mine to possess nothing of our own under the sun».

Such poverty leads to obedience, and Francis taught «that he has never perfectly renounced the world who keeps hidden in his heart the treasure of his own will». He himself pursued obedience as others pursue power. «The brothers placed themselves in the service of perfect obedience, as soon as an order was given they hastened to obey, not questioning whether it were just or unjust, accepting it as the will of God; and therefore it was sweet to them». Francis went still further for he said: «Holy obedience makes a man subject to all the men in the world, and not to men alone, but also to all beasts and wild animals so that they may do with him whatsoever they will in so far as it is granted to them by the Lord».

This obedience had two twin sisters, simplicity, and an unbounded trust in the loving providence of God, a confidence in the charity of fellow men, the children of God. When the Twelve got back to the valley of Spoleto Francis seems to have realized that the time had come when they must have a fixed home, and the first shelter that offered itself was a shed at Rivo Torto not far from the Leper hospital. During those months Otto IV, Frederick's rival for the imperial crown, passed along the valley of Spoleto on his way to Rome. Francis sent one of the brothers to warn him of the evanescence of all earthly dignity. In two years Otto had lost his crown, and Francis' warning would have been remembered and quoted.

Rivo Torto was destined to be only a passing home, and the brothers left after a very uncivil peasant drove his ass

Saint Clare

in declaring his right to the place. It was then that the abbot of San Benedetto, the Benedictine monastery on Monte Subasio to whom the Porziuncula belonged, offered it to Francis as a home for the Fraternity on condition that it should always be considered the mother church of the order. And Lady Poverty was not slighted by deed of gift for each year Francis sent the Abbot a basket of fish as rent, and received in return a flask of oil as the Abbot's receipt.

No home could have been more according to Francis' wish, first of all because it was a sanctuary of Our Lady. He loved her as his Mother, his Lady, his Queen, the Mother and Queen of every soul and every creature, above all as the Mother of Christ, and he never tired of improvising songs in her honour.

Thus the Porziuncula came to have almost a sacramental meaning to the Fraternity which is best expressed in a story which tells how soon after the Brothers were settled there, someone had a vision of the little chapel surrounded by a crowd of blind people who were all imploring God for sight. Francis was in their midst also praying, and the prayers were heard and all those blind eyes were opened. We catch glimpses of the Brothers life of service and prayer for besides reciting the Breviary - always providing they had the necessary books - they were continually bursting into songs of praise; praise of God, of Christ, of the Blessed Virgin and all the saints and angels, praises for and through all God's creatures. Those who knew Francis told how «he was always occupied with Jesus. Jesus he carried in his heart, Jesus in his mouth, Jesus in his eyes, Jesus in his hands, Jesus in all his members. Often he forgot where he was and what he was doing at the thought of Jesus, and with such glowing love was he moved towards Jesus Christ, yea, and with such intimate love did his Beloved repay this, that it seemed to the servant of God himself that he felt his Saviour almost continually before his eyes».

Everything spoke to Francis of his Beloved: Christ the corner-stone, Christ the lamb of God, Christ the Light of the

Altar of the Porziuncula

world, Christ the Water of life, Christ the bread and Wine of life, Christ the Vine, Christ the Way. All day long and in every place, he had Christ before his eyes. He could hardly bear to put out a candle, or see bread wasted, or water polluted, all for love of Jesus. He wanted a plot of land set aside for the cultivation of our «brothers the flowers so that all who see them shall remember the eternal sweetness». Christ the creating Word was in every creature, shining in all beauty, Christ the Pilgrim met him in every stranger, Christ the crucified in each sufferer, the risen Christ in all life.

The Pope had given the Brothers permission to preach penance; and those days a clear line was drawn between this kind of preaching and the theological exposition of dogma. The preaching of penance exactly suited Francis in whose mouth it became an exhortation to love. Not long after the brothers were settled at the Porziuncula, the Bishop invited him to preach in the church of San Giorgio and in the cathedral. Crowds flocked to see the former king of the revels, now penniless and ragged; they hung on the words and on his wonderful voice, and they knew that he and his brothers practised what they preached. These men had the right to preach the beauty of poverty since they lived it; a right to exhort others to charity since their chief care was for the worst cases among the lepers; the right to cry «peace», since they were at peace with all men for the love of God. Listeners at various times reported: «He began to preach wonderfully of despising the world, and of holy penance and voluntary poverty, of the desire for the kingdom of God, and of the self-stripping of Christ in His passion... he seemed to those who beheld him as a man from another world, whose heart was set on heaven, and his face turned upwards towards it seeking to draw others with him». No wonder people listened!

The Three Companions tell «how all Assisi wept tears of compassion over the passion of Christ, and nobles and plebeians, clerics and layfolk threw aside the thought of passing things to walk in the way Francis showed them».

Basilica of Santa Chiara

At that moment the chief trouble in Assisi was again the acute rivalry between the «Majores» and «Minores», and there was great topical significance in Francis' choice of the title «Minores» for himself and his brothers. Here was a living example of men who deliberately wished to be the «Lesser Brothers», the Friars Minor, and asked only for the privilege to be «humble and subject to all». It gave new meaning to the greeting of peace, and for Francis peace is a gift from Christ which Christians hold in trust. The practical effect of Francis' influence was that the treaty of civic peace which had been drafted in 1203 was ratified in 1210.

Among those who listened to Francis was Chiara, Clare, the daughter of Favorone a feudal noble and his wife Ortolana. These «people were rich in all that the world holds riches»: Clare was a beautiful girl of sixteen, and her family were bent on her making a great marriage...

However «she would in no way be persuaded». She must certainly have followed each step of Francis' career, and he had heard of her for indeed her name was on all lips on account of her beauty, her goodness and her position.

Her cousin Ruffino had already joined the Fraternity, and he may have acted as a link and Francis «God's huntsman was minded to snatch this noble booty from the world and to offer it to his Master. And so he visited her, and many times she visited him, coming forth from her home in secret with an intimate female friend secretly so that no one should see her». In these meetings Clare listened to Francis «with the utmost fervour whenever he spoke of the love of Jesus... and enlightened by the flaming torch of his speech, she caught as it were a glimpse of the Beatific Vision. Forthwith the things of this world seemed to her as dung, and dreading the allurements of the flesh, she resolved to lay aside any thought of earthly marriage, and to do her utmost to make herself worthy as the bride of the Heavenly King, and henceforward she regarded blessed Francis, as, after God, the charioteer of her soul». Clare's mind was now made up, and «as it drew to Palm Sunday the girl Clare came to Francis in ardent expecta-

Sermon to the birds

tion wishing to know how and when her conversion could be finally accomplished: and he commanded her that, dressed in her habitual clothes, she should go as usual to receive the blessed palm with all the faithful. In the following night she would set out from her home and turn from the joys of the world to weep for the Passion of Christ. When therefore it came to Palm Sunday, she appeared among the women resplendent for the joy that was in her, and merrily she entered the church with her companions. There, according to God's providence it befell that when the moment came for all to approach the altar and receive the blessed olive, Clare was held back by shyness. Seeing this the Bishop came down the steps to where she was and put the palm in her hand... In the following night having prepared herself to obey the Saint's command she fled from her father's house with one trusted companion, and not wishing to leave by the chief door, with miraculous strength she opened the side door which was heavily barred with stones and wooden beams. Thus she left family, home and city, and with great fervour went to Santa Maria degli Angeli where the friars were keeping watch and singing the divine praises».

Before the altar of the Porziuncula Clare made her profession: «I want only Jesus Christ, and to live by the Gospel owning nothing, and in chastity». To seal this vow Francis cut off her long fair hair, and in the place of her fine clothes he gave her the rough habit of poverty with the white veil of chastity and the coarse black one of penance. After this he took her to the Benedictine convent at Bastia. The Bishop must at least have been a party to all this: without his tacit consent Francis would never have dared to act as he did.

When Clare's flight was discovered, the fury of her family was like a whirlwind: with «their hearts torn and greatly disapproving» the men besieged the convent, and used every means to make her «renounce this dishonour which is bringing shame on our family, and has no equal in the whole neighbourhood». Clare defended herself by clinging

Wolf of Gubbio

49

to the altar of the chapel and at last she uncovered her shorn head; crestfallen they turned away.

Francis then moved Clare to another Benedictine convent of Sant'Angelo in Panzo on the slopes of Monte Subasio: and within a short time she was joined by her younger sister Agnes. Again the family stormed: they entered the convent courtyard demanding that Agnes should be handed over to them; she answered that she would never leave her sister, They dragged her to the gate screaming for help, Clare fell on her knees, and those strong men were unable to lift the fifteen-year old girl; they had to give it up and leave.

Not long after this the Bishop gave Francis the church of San Damiano to be the home of the Second Franciscan Order, generally known as that of the Poor Clares. Francis was their guide and father. For him every woman was the bride of Christ, still more anyone vowed to the service of God, and he would not even call Clare by her Christian name, but referred to her as «Christian Woman».

Eventually she was joined by her mother and various relations as well as by numerous followers; and for fortytwo years she defended Francis' ideals with unswerving loyalty. She loved Poverty as he did, with the same vision, and he had kindled in her heart a twin flame of the love of God from that which burned in his own. In her he saw the perfect reflection of his ideal. San Damiano became a twin sanctuary to the Porziuncula, and Clare loved to describe herself as «the little plant which our Father Francis planted in the garden of poverty». Even during Francis' lifetime his prophecy about San Damiano was fulfilled.

ST. FRANCIS' PORTRAIT
(1212-1215)

Meanwhile the fame of the Fraternity was fast increasing, and for a moment Francis again hesitated. Was it his duty to be always travelling and the constant centre of a crowd? Could he not serve God in a life of prayer and penance in a remote hermitage as already some of the brothers were doing? He was immensely attracted to such a vocation which he called the «life of angels», and yet so fearful of self-will that he sent Masseo to Clare and also to Sylvester asking them to decide what he should do. When Masseo told him how, separately, and after long prayer both Clare and Sylvester had declared that his vocation was to give to others what he had himself received.

Francis accepted the decision unquestioningly, «Let us go forth with God» he replied. They set out immediately and between Cannara and Bevagna came on a multitude of birds some in the trees, some on the ground. «And when Saint Francis saw this the Spirit of God came over him, and he bade his disciples wait saying: «I am going to preach to our sisters the birds». And he walked into the field to where the birds were sitting: and as soon as he began to preach the birds who were in the trees flew down and none of them moved, although he went right among them, so that his cowl touched several of them...

Saint Francis said to the birds: «My sister birds! You owe God great gratitude, and ought always and everywhere to praise and exalt Him because you can fly so freely wherever you please, and for your double and triple clothing, and for your coloured and most beautiful coat, and for the food you do not have to work for, and for the lovely voices your Creator has given you... God gives you rivers and springs to drink from, and hills and mountains, cliffs and rocks in which to hide, and high trees to build your nests in, and though you neither spin nor weave He gives you and your young ones the necessary clothing. Therefore you must greatly love the Creator since He has given you such blessings. Watch well my sister birds that you be not ungrateful, and busy yourselves always in praising God.

After our holy Father's words all those little birds began to open their beaks, and beat their wings, and stretch out their necks and bow their heads reverently to the earth, and with their song and their movements they showed that his words had greatly pleased them. And when he this, Saint Francis rejoiced in spirit, and wondered over so many birds and over their variety and differences and that they were so tame; and he praised the Creator for it and gently exhorted them to praise the Creator themselves.

When he had finished his sermon and exhortation to praise God, he made the sign of the cross over all the birds, and at once they flew up, twittering wonderfully and strongly, and separating, flew away».

All Francis' life was a breaking down of barriers, a reaching out into the mysteries of creation, through love. The preaching to the birds was repeated in many places; wherever he went he made animal friends, and alway he spoke to them in the same tone: «Sing my sisters, cicala and praise the Lord thy Creator with a joyful song». He tamed everything he met, and the best known story is that of the wolf of Gubbio. Peasants warned him that the hills were infested with wolves, to which Francis replied: «What harm have I done to my brothers the wolves that they should eat me and the ass? I will go on in the name of God».

When he reached Gubbio he went out in search of the special wolf who was terrifying the neighbourhood, and brought him back into the city where he became the pet of everyone.

Celano eloquently describes Fracis' attitude to all creature: «His gentle love and charity were extended to dumb and senseless creatures, to birds and beasts, to every sentient thing and even to insensible objects... it is indeed wonderfull how even the irrational creatures were aware of his loving kindness and reciprocated his tenderness... He would cause honey and the best wine to be given to the bees so that they should not suffer during the winter. Their nimble activity and wonderful science could move him to glorifying the wonders of the Lord so enthusiastically that he would often speak of nothing else for a whole day... and when he considered the glory of the flowers how happy he was in gazing on their beauty, and enjoying their fragrance! How easily his spirit would take wing to meditate on the beauty of that unique flower as

Portrait of Saint Francis (Cimabue

fair as the approaching spring which growing from the Root of Jesse brought new life to countless men whose souls were dead... his tenderness embraced even the worms for he had read of Our Saviour «I am a worm and no man». Therefore he would pick up the worms from the road and put them in a safe place so that passers-by should not tread them underfoot... When he found many flowers growing together he would speak to them and encourage them, as though they could understand, to praise the Lord. It was the same with the fields of corn and the vineyards, the stones of the earth and in the woods, all the fair meadows, the rippling brooks, the spouting gardens, earth, fire, air and wind - all these in his pure childlike spirit he exhorted to love God and serve Him joyfully». He was wont to call all created things his brothers and sisters, and in a wonderful manner, inaccessible to others he would enter into the secret of things as one to whom had been given the glorious liberty of the children of God».

Celano continues his portrait of Francis: «How fair, radiant and glorious was the sinlessness of his life, the simplicity of his words, the purity of his heart, his love of God and of his neighbour, his unquestioning obedience and his fidelity to his Master! To this must be added his angelic appearance, the charm of his manner, his natural gentleness, the kindliness of his conversation, the delicacy of his admonitions, the loyalty with which he treated anything told him in confidence, the wisdom of counsel, the energy of his actions and his general loveableness.

He was a man of great eloquence; the expression of his face was gay and kindly, equally free of torpor as of arrogance. He was of moderate stature, rather small, his head of moderate size and round, his face rather long and narrow, his forehead low and smooth, his dark eyes of moderate size, friendly and candid; his hair dark, his ears small and close to the head, his temples smooth. His speech was captivating, fiery and spiritual, his voice powerful, pleasant and harmonious, his teeth were white

Wooden Crucifix 15th century

and close together behind narrow, gently rounded lips, his beard dark and rather sparse, his neck slender resting on straight shoulders, his arms short with delicate hands and long fingers and nails, his spare fragile body with its slender legs and small feet was covered in a rough tunic. He was slow to anger, swift to forgive, absorbed in contemplation, assiduous in prayer, always consistent. He had a quick intelligence, a reliable memory, and was subtle in argument, prudent in decision, and simple in everything. In his great humility he showed himself mild with all; wisely conforming himself to the manners of others. Among saints he was the saintliest, among sinners as one of themselves».

Such was the man who conquered pratically everyone he met whether robbers or wordlings, princes or beggars, the respectable and the disreputable.

There is the famous story of Masseo who, after one of Francis's amazingly successful sermons asked him: «I wonder why the whole world runs after thee more than others, and all men want to see and hear and obey thee? Thou art not fair of body, thou art not deeply learned, thou art not of noble birth: why does the whole world run after thee?».

When Saint Francis heard this, he rejoiced, and turned his eyes to Heaven, and stood a long time thus with his soul lifted up to God, and when he came to himself, he knelt down and gave thanks and praise to God, and turning to Brother Masseo, said with great spiritual power: «Dost thou wish to know why this happens to me? I know it from the all-highest God Who sees the good and bad in all the earth. His most holy eyes have nowhere seen a greater, a more miserable, poorer sinner than I. Because in the whole world he found no more wretched being to do the wonderful work He wishes done, therefore He has chosen me, so as to put to shame the noble and the great, strength and beauty and wordly wisdom; that all may know that power and virtue come from Him alone, and not from any creature, and that no one can exalt themselves before His face».

Extasis of St. Francis (Giotto)

Lower Church

A typical incident is that of the Lord Orlando of Chiusi. Francis and a brother passed by his castle one day while a feast was going on. Unhesitatingly Francis knocked at the door; he asked leave to speak, and his text to the assembled guests was: «So great is the good that awaits me in Heaven, that all suffering here is sweet». The audience was conquered, especially Lord Orlando, but Francis refused to speak to him privately until the feast was ended. The result was that Lord Orlando gave him the mountain of Alvernia in the range between the Tiber and Arno valleys which became his favourite retreat.

Wherever Francis went he always showed the utmost reverence for priests, and would never speak in a Church without the permission of the priest or bishop. In one place where he was speaking in the market place, the people pointed out the priest as a notorius evil liver.

Francis went and knelt before him: «I do not know whether he is good or bad: for me he is good». He declared that if he met a priest and an angel, he would kiss the priest's hand before saluting the angel, «because that hand had consecrated and touched the very Body of Our Lord».

Devotion to the Blessed Sacrament was at the centre of his heart; he spoke of it over and over again, and we feel how he felt the insufficiency of his words. «Kissing your feet, I implore you all my brothers, and with the utmost affection I beseech you to show the greatest possible reverence and honour to the most holy Body and Blood of our Lord Jesus Christ... Consider your dignity O Brothers who are priests, and be holy because He is holy... It is a great misfortune and a miserable fault to have Him thus near you, and to be thinking of anything else. Let the whole man be seized with dread; let the whole world tremble; let the heavens exult when Christ, the Son of the living God is on the altar in the hands of the priest. O amazing splendour and astounding condescension! O sublime humility! O humble sublimity! The Master of the universe, God Himself and Son of God humbles Himself so far as to hide Himself for our salvation under the feeble appearance of bread! See brothers the humility of God... keep nothing of yourselves for yourselves, so that He may possess you entirely, who has given Himself wholly for you».

Francis considered it an almost unpardonable sin to miss Mass voluntarily; he received Holy Communion very often «and with such devotion that he enkindled the souls of others... he was as it were spiritually inebriated, and frequently wrapt in ecstasy». One day a rather worldly friend asked him: «Father what do you do during those long hours before the Blessed Sacrament?». «My son in return I ask you what does the poor man do at the rich man's door, the sick man in presence of his physician, the thirsty man at a limpid stream? What they do, I do before the Eucharistic God. I pray. I adore. I love».

If he were prevented from being present at Mass, he would have the Gospel of the day read to him; in his own words: «If I cannot assist at Mass I adore the Body of Christ in meditation, and with the eyes of the soul, just as if I were present during the Mass». Saint Bonaventure describes Francis at prayer: «One night he was seen praying with his hands extended in the shape of a cross, his entire body raised from the ground and surrounded with a luminous mist, the marvellous light round his body bearing witness to the wonderful illumination of his spirit. By certain indications one could recognize that hidden secrets of divine wisdom were revealed to him. Nevertheless he did not reveal them to others unless urged to by Christian charity. When he returned from his private devotions, during which he was apt to be actually transformed into a different man, his chief concern was to behave in a most ordinary fashion. He often said to his familiars: «When a servant of God experiences a divine visitation in prayer he must say: Thou hast sent this consolation to me a sinner O Lord, and I commit it to Thy custody, for I feel that I am a thief of Thy treasures».

He preferred lonely and deserted place and churches for solitary prayers just because he did not want to be observed; and often his disciples knew that he was terribly tempted and assaulted by the devil who was determined to distract him; his refuge was to turn to Christ with the plea «Hide me under the shadow of Thy wings».

Some of his penances were known to his friends; he had been seen rolling in the rose bushes at the Porziuncola; seen building up snow figures when tempted by some natural desire of affection, heard telling himself that they were his wife, his children, his servants; «they are dying of cold, hurry up and give them clothes»! And if you cannot, then be glad that you have no one to serve but God alone. His whole daily life was a penance, but none could know the unyielding ferocity with which he pursued self-will and

St. Clare and St. Elisabeth of Hungary (S. Martini)

selfishness into the inmost recesses of his own being, and never rested till he had cast them out. He was always clearing away the rubbish in himself, and opening new windows through which the light of God could stream in. Because of his love of the Blessed Sacrament, Francis wanted everything in a church to be beautiful; and the door of the tabernacle to be of gold. He could not bear for any church to be shabby or neglected, and would at once wish to clean and adorn it. On one occasion when he was sweeping out a country church a peasant came in; he went out a Friar Minor.

Francis' radius of activity was constantly increasing; within a few years the friars became known all over Italy, but Francis' own mind had leaped on another stage and he was dreaming of missions and martyrdom.

Only a few months after Clare's conversion he had set out for Syria; but the boat was driven on to the Dalmatian coast and Francis and his brothers found it very difficult to get back to Italy. Eventually they were hidden in the hold of a ship, but before the Adriatic was crossed Francis had made friends with all on board, and as usual was holding his audience enthralled.

The next year he started for Spain, meaning to cross from there to Morocco and if possible be martyred: «He seemed like one intoxicated, so eagerly did he press forward». But it was no use; he fell ill in Spain, and when he was able to move, reluctantly he turned homeward, feeling that his immediate duty was to the brothers in Italy.

THE FOUNDATION OF THE THIRD ORDER
(1215-1217)

Francis was again in Rome for the Fourth Lateran Council when Innocent formally recognized the Franciscan friars. The Pope made a stirring appeal for reform within the Church, for the sign of the cross in the soul and life of every Christian, and for the Crusade which appeared more possible since the Moorish defeat at Las Navas three

Francis preaches to Honorius III (Giotto)

years previously. He made much of the example of the Children's Crusade, that heroic and pitiful venture in which thousands of children lost their lives, and which vividly illustrates the division between the mediaeval mentality and our own. Could men remain indifferent when children were so prompt in sacrifice, asked Innocent, and he must have been aware that some of his listeners were prepared for any enterprise.

One result of the Pope's appeal was Francis' Letter to All Christians in which he reaches out to the masses he would never know personally but who mattered to him so much. It is addressed to the Christian world in general, and to every individual, and lays down the well known Christian principles with tremendous force and vitality, and through quotations from the Gospels. Above all it demands a new realisation of the meaning of the Christ life. Francis had already acquired a large, loose following of men and women outside the fraternity; it was not uncommon for a whole village to wish to be considered his disciples. Among the more prominent of these followers were Lucchesio and Buonadonna of Poggibonsi, and the rich Roman lady Jacopa de' Settesoli who became such a friend to the Order that Francis nicknamed her «Brother Jacopa». At first the Letter to All Christians, and their own enthusiasm provided the «rule» for this outer circle of friends, and several years elapsed before Francis realized that a more definite organization was necessary. Thus arose the Order of Penance, commonly called the Third Order of Saint Francis, and it numbers many saints among its members, and has sanctified, and does sanctify thousands of humble lives. Only God knows how many souls it has lifted out of the mud of selfishness into the clear air of charity. The crumbs were always as precious to Francis as the loaves.

While living in the world the members of this outer circle have as their elder brothers the Friars, and the Poor Clares as their sisters; they have the privilege and the responsibility of wearing the Franciscan badge in which the arm of Christ is crossed with the arm of Francis in an eloquent symbol of what the Franciscan vocation means. Each one too has the right to remember a window in the Basilica of Saint Francis in Assisi where Francis has his hand on the shoulder of a kneeling follower whom he is presenting to Our Lord.

The gradual formation of the Third Order was a great extension of the Fraternity and its roots lay in the depths of Francis' love of souls. Men, just ordinary men can seldom have been loved, trusted, an appreciated as they were by him: he could always be relied on to see the best in everyone, and each single human being was dear to him because Christ had died to save that particular person. Like children asking for safety we pray, «within Thy wounds hide me», but Francis, in whom nothing was perfunctory, and everything was incandescent and dynamic, found in those wounds the overwhelming realisation of the love of Christ, and of the horrible reality of sin. Each sight of a crucifix strengthened his longing for souls, and it was to find renewed expression in the granting of the Porziuncula indulgence in 1216.

While Innocent III lay dying in Perugia, one night Francis left the sleeping brothers and went into the chapel of the Porziuncula. As he prayed, Our Lord bade him ask for a plenary indulgence for every person who should visit the chapel with true contrition for sin. He made his petition to Honorius III who was elected Pope two days after Innocent's death, asking for an indulgence to be attached to the Porziuncula without the obligation of any offering. The Pope enquired how many years Francis wished for but he replied «Holy Father, I am asking for souls, not years, and I ask in the name of Christ, who sent me». At first Honorius demurred for the demand was unusual, but at last he repeated twice, «It is my will that you have what you seek».

This decision met with warm opposition from the Papal court and the cardinals pointed out that such an indulgence, granted to a shrine in Italy, would seriously prejudice the indulgences of the Crusade and of the tombs of the Apostles in Rome. Honorius would not retract his promise, but he consented to limit the Porziuncula indulgence to the feast of the consecration of the chapel which was fixed for August 2nd.

As Francis turned away the Pope called him back; did he want no document signed and sealed to prove the validity of the privilege he had been given? «Holy Father» he answered, and there is a smile in the words, «Your word is sufficient to me. If this is the work of God it is for Him to manifest His work. I want no document. The Blessed virgin shall be the charter, and Christ the Notary, and the angels shall be the witnesses». The Porziuncula indulgence has always rested on this verbal assurance.

Seven bishops took part in the consecration of the little church of Saint Mary of the Angels. Francis was asked to preach, and after telling the story of the indulgence he went on, «I want to send you all to Heaven». He could not have described his own activity better.

The first foreign comment on the Order is also dated 1216, and it comes from the French Bishop Jacques de Vitry who was visiting the Papal court at Perugia. He wrote: «During the time I spent at the curia I saw much that entirely dissatisfied me: all were so taken up with worldly and temporal affairs, with politics and law, that it was hardly possible to speak of what was spiritual.

One thing however comforted me in these surroundings. Many men and women, some of them rich and worldly, for Christ's sake have forsaken everything and have fled from the world. They are called Friars Minor, and stand in high repute both with the Pope and Cardinals. They do not heed temporal things, but work day in and out with zeal and diligence to draw souls away from the vanities of the world, to save them from falling and to carry them along with themselves».

Bishop Jacques came to the Porziuncula, «and when he saw how poorly the brothers lived, and that they slept upon straw and ate off the bare earth he was so overcome that he broke into tears and cried: «How will it go with us who live so luxuriously day after day in superfluity and delights?».

THE CHAPTER AT PENTECOST 1217
(1217-1219)

Hitherto the brothers had seen the world through Francis' eyes; he was their leader and their law, but the time was coming when the life of the Fraternity would touch the world at too many points to remain itself untouched. Francis was beginning to pay the price of his own tremendous success; and it began to be obvious that the «rule» which had easily sufficed for twelve like-minded men would not always suffice for thousands, who, moreover were beyond the range of Francis' personal influence. The idea of organization had raised its head and it was alien to Francis. Could such inspiration as his be «organized» in the accepted sense of the term? And yet the spirit, free as air, has to accept some formal scheme when it comes to directing the lives of a crowd of men. A Chapter was held at the Porziuncola at Pentecost 1217 and the Brothers came from all over Italy and already too from other countries. With what anticipation they must have walked through the spring woods and fields, and many were to see Francis for the first time. How they must have tiptoed to see him when he rose to preach of what it meant to be a Friar Minor. How many of them turned to their companions: «Yes, it's worth it, we haven't been deceived».

Two matters had been listed for prayer and consideration: the appointment of Provincial Ministers, and the sending of Brothers to establish provinces of the Fraternity outside Italy. The first subject was the most important in that it implied an innovation. Superiors in the ordinary sense could never fit into the Fraternity, and Francis' own wish was to be «the servant of all»; the head of any Franciscan community was to take the place of the mother of a family, and these «mothers» came to be called «Ministers» or «Guardians», never «Superiors». The Ministers were to tend their brothers as a shepherd does his sheep, «often visiting them, instructing and encouraging them, and on their side the brothers must obey the Minister in all things that are not contrary to the life of a Friar Minor... «Between the Ministers and the Brothers this shall be the rule of conduct: Whatsoever you will that men should do unto you, that do you to them», and Francis went on to warn the «Minister-servants» that should any Brother be lost through them, «they will have to render an account to Our Lord Jesus Christ». He repeated his injunctions, «let no one ask from another more than he is himself ready to give to God», and to one Minister he wrote: «Let there be no brother in the world who, if he has sinned, no matter how grievously, having seen thy face shall not go away assured of thy mercy. If he does not ask mercy, ask him if he desires it, and if he should appear before thee a thousand times, love him more than me; to the end thou mayest draw him to the Lord... those who are set over others must never pride themselves on their offices more than if they were set to wash their brothers feet; woe to any religious who in a place of authority does not wish to give it up; blessed the Superior who in the midst of his subjects comports himself as though they were his masters».

Provincial Ministers were elected for the seven provinces of Italy, but what really stirred the Brothers was the idea of foreign missions. It was decided to establish provinces in France, Spain, Portugal, Germany and Hungary; probably in Syria too, and that very important province was entrusted to the extremely efficient Brother Elias.

Francis could not bear to be left behind; in this as in everything he must be the example for all the Brothers, «so will the Brothers be encouraged to endure adversities patiently, knowing that I do the same». He bade them all pray that he might choose the right province, and when they returned he exclaimed: «I choose the province, of France because there more than anywhere Catholics show a special reverence for the Body of Christ». He took leave of the Brothers with the words: «Go forth in the name of the Lord in all humility and modesty... pray to the Lord in your hearts and speak no idle or useless words. Though you walk abroad let your conduct be as humble and becoming as in a hermitage. Indeed wherever we travel we have our cell always with us. Brother Body is our

Allegory of Lady Poverty and Chastity (Giotto) 69

cell, and the soul is the hermit who dwells therein to pray and meditate on the Lord. Of little use is a cell made with hands if the soul is not at rest in its own cell».

Before starting for France, Francis wished to make a pilgrimage to Rome and Brother Masseo went with him. They came to a small town, and having nothing they started to beg, taking separate streets. «Now Masseo being tall and handsome had many good and large pieces of bread given him, yea, entire loaves; but because Francis was a man of mean appearance, and small of stature and accounted a vile beggar by those who did not know him, he received nothing but a few mouthfuls and crumbs of dry bread... When they had begged enough they went to a place outside the town where there was a fair fountain, and also a broad, convenient stone on which each put the alms he had received.

Seeing that the pieces of bread of Brother Masseo were larger and better than his own Francis was filled with joy and said: O Brother Masseo we are not worthy of such treasures». When he had repeated this several times Masseo replied: «Father how can this be called a treasure when we are so poor and lack the most necessary things, we who have neither cloths nor knives, nor plates, nor porringer, house, table, man or maid servant?». Then said Saint Francis: «This is what I call great treasure: that there is nothing here provided by human industry, but everything is given us by Divine Providence, as we see in this bread we have begged, in this stone which serves so beautifully as a table, and in this clear fountain. Therefore let us pray to God that we may love holy Poverty with all our heart, for Poverty is so noble that God Himself was made subject to it». When they had prayed and eaten and drunk of the bread and water, they rose and went their way... After a time they came to a church, and Francis said, «Let us go in and pray». He went behind the altar and his soul was so inflamed with love of holy Poverty «that the increased colour of his face, and the unusual movement of his lips made it seem as though he were breathing out flames of love». He turned to Masseo: «Ah,

Allegory of Obedience and St. Francis in glory   71

ah, ah Brother Masseo yield thyself to me»: at the third repetition of these words he lifted Masseo by his breath into the air and threw him a spear's length which greatly astonished Masseo. Brother Masseo said that during the time he was thrown by Saint Francis' breath, he tasted such spiritual consolation in the Holy Spirit that in all his life he had never felt the like».

Francis never reached France: in Florence on the way north he met Cardinal Ugolino, Bishop of Ostia, and that meeting too was a milestone. The Cardinal was then over sixty, a great noble, a great churchman, a handsome man who lived like an ascetic, and had always admired the Franciscan movement. From the moment they met the two men became friends: Ugolino knew that Francis' enemies were only waiting for an opportune moment to try and destroy his work; he, on the contrary was determined to help him steer clear of the waiting shoals. He persuaded Francis that, at the moment he was more necessary in Italy than in France: he himself took an early opportunity of visiting Clare at Saint Damiano, and his subsequent letters show how deep was his sympathy for their ideals. In Rome his house was always open to the Brothers, and when Francis stayed there he insisted on going out to beg as usual. At first Ugolino demurred, would Francis not honour his house by eating his bread? But Francis replied that the Cardinal's house was more honoured by respecting Lady Poverty and Ugolino fell in with his guest's wishes: «Do as seems well to thee my son for God is with thee». The incident shows the quality of their friendship.

During the months after the missionaries departure Francis went up and down the country as usual, everywhere gaining new followers. Later he was to head the Friars' Rule with the words: «Whoever comes to the brethren, friend or enemy, thief, or robber shall be kindly received». He himself had always put this principle into practise, and the practical side of such kindness had been vividly illustrated by an episode at the hermitage of Monte Casale. The Brothers there confronted him with the question whether or not it was desirable to give alms to robbers. Francis replied: «If you do as I say, then in God I hope to save their souls. Take good bread and wine out to them in the woods calling: Brother Robbers come here; we are Brothers, and bring you good wine and bread. They will come at once, and then I will spread a cloth on the ground and wait on them with humility and cheerfulness while they eat. Afterwards I will speak to them of God, and will beg them in God's name to promise not to kill or harm anyone. If you ask everything of them at once they will say «No», but because of your humility and kindness, they will grant this request».

The next day in recognition of their good intentions you shall take them bread and wine, eggs and fruit, and wait on them while they eat. Then you may say: «Why do you wander about all day and suffer hunger enduring much while in thought and deed you perpetrate many things and thus imperil your souls. It is much better to serve God, Who will give you what you need on earth, and at the same time you shall save your souls». And for the sake of your humility and goodness the Lord will grant that our Brother Robbers may be converted». Another version of the story is even more forcible: because the Guardian of the convent had driven the robbers away with scorn, he was sent to search for them over «mountain and valley», «then thou shalt kneel down before them and humbly beg their forgiveness for thy rudeness and severity». In any case the robbers were converted, and several of them entered the Fraternity.

There is another episode which strikes a deeper note, and which Francis desired Brother Leo to write down. It comes straight from his heart to each of his lovers. Tradition says that he and Leo were walking from Perugia to Santa Maria degli Angeli, one biting day in early spring. Leo was walking ahead and heard Francis call: «O Brother Leo although the Friars Minor give a good and edifying example of sanctity, note and write down that this is not Perfect Joy».

After they had gone a little further Francis called out

again: «O Brother Leo, even if a Friar Minor should give sight to the blind, make the crooked straight, cast out devils, restore hearing to the deaf, make the lame walk, and the dumb to speak, and even more raise up a man dead for days, write that in none of these things is Perfect Joy».
Going on again Saint Francis called out loudly: «O Brother Leo, if a Friar Minor possessed every language and science and the whole of the Scriptures; if he could prophecy and reveal not only the future, but the secrets of conscience and the soul, write that Perfect Joy is not in this».
Passing on a little further, Saint Francis again called out loudly: «Brother Leo, little lamb of God even if a Friar Minor should speak with the tongue of an angel and know the course of the stars and the virtues of the herbs, even if all the treasure of the earth had been revealed to him and he knew the qualities of the birds, the fish and all animals, of men and trees, of stones and roots and waters, write that Perfect Joy is not in this».
Going on again Saint Francis called loudly: «O Brother Leo, even if a Friar Minor could preach so eloquently that he converted all infidels to the faith of Christ, write that Perfect Joy is not in this».
Thus he spoke for the best part of two miles, until Brother Leo, in great amazement questioned him saying: «For God's sake Father, I beseech you tell me in what does Perfect Joy consist?».
And Saint Francis answered thus:
«When we come to Saint Mary of the Angels drenched with rain, numb with cold, covered with mud and tormented with hunger, and when we knock at the gate and the porter comes and asks: «Who are you?» and we answer «Two of your brothers» hereupon he retorts «You are lying, a pair of scoundrels who wander round deceiving people, and robbing alms from the poor; away with you». and if he then refuses to open and leaves us standing in the snow and rain, shivering and hungry till night: then if we endure so much abuse and cruelty patiently and calmly without murmuring, thinking with humility and charity that this porter knows us as we really are, and that God

makes him turn thus against us, O Brother Leo write that herein is Perfect Joy. And if we persevere and go on knocking, and he comes out with anger and chases us away like importunate vagabonds with insults and blows saying: «Get away from here you good-for-nothing thieves, get you gone to the poor house, for here there is neither lodging nor food for you», to endure this patiently, with gladness and good humour, O Brother Leo, herein is Perfect Joy. And if we, constrained by hunger, cold and darkness, continue knocking and weeping loudly, and entreat him for the love of God to open the door and let us in, and if he, being still more enraged cries: «These are importunate rascals, I will treat them as they deserve», and rushing out with a knotted stick: seizes us by our cowls, throws us down, rolls us in the snow, and beats us with every knot of that stick: if we, thinking of the sufferings of Our blessed Lord, endure all these things gladly and patiently, bearing them for love of Him, O Brother Leo, write that herein is Perfect Joy. And now hearken to this conclusion: above all grace and gifts of the Holy Spirit which Christ gives to His friends, is that of overcoming oneself and for love of Christ gladly bearing pain, insults, disgrace and hardships. For we cannot glory in any of the other gifts of God, for they are not ours but God's... wherefore the Apostle says: «God forbid that I should glory save in the cross of Our Lord Jesus Christ to Whom be honour and glory, world without end. Amen».

Meanwhile the missionaries were faring very badly. In France, Portugal, Hungary and Germany they were taken for heretics, and wandered about miserably as vagrants, not knowing a word of any foreign language, or having any idea of the conditions in other countries. «Thus straitened and afflicted, compelled to flee from divers provinces, sometimes robbed and beaten as thieves, they returned to Blessed Francis in great bitterness of spirit». Naturally these experiences were discussed, and a certain latent dissatisfaction with Francis' simplicity began to find expression. He sent his disciples out to conquer the world for Christ by their example, their poverty, charity, joy and peace. They were to bind up the wounds of humanity, to comfort, never to judge: he insisted that others whom they saw living in luxury were not to be despised: «God is also their Master; He can call them when He wills and make them just and holy». Above all the missionaries were to set out without any credentials from the Holy See, armed only with the cross and the Gospel. The chief danger lay in the lack of credentials, and undoubtedly the Cardinal had the majority of the brothers with him when he advised that for the future every missionary must carry credentials. In 1210 another gathering of Friars was held at the Porziuncula to which five thousand Friars came. The title Chapter of Mats was probably first applied to this gathering, though for other chapters also the Brothers may have had to lodge in wattle huts; there was certainly no other accommodation available. Francis had returned from a preaching journey to find that the Assisans had started to build a large stone house for the convenience of the chapter: he was outraged by such an insult to Lady Poverty in her own sanctuary. He climbed on to the roof and started to demolish it, and was only deterred when messengers arrived from the civic authorities saying that the building belonged to them and not to him.

Cardinal Ugolino presided over the meeting, and Francis eloquently repeated all he had been saying for the last ten years. He would not even allow any plans to be made for feeding the five thousand brothers, but his trust was justified and abundant supplies flowed in from all the neighbourhood. Even then some voices were raised in doubt as to whether a large community could exist with no practical provision for daily needs. Francis replied in bitter grief: «My Brothers, my Brothers! The Lord has called me in simplicity and humility, and He pointed out this way for myself and for those who are willing to believe in me and follow me... The Lord told me that He willed me to be poor and foolish in this world, and that He willed not to lead us by any way other than that knowledge. But with this learning and wisdom of yours, may the Lord confound you, and

The challenge before the Sultan

I trust in the Castellans of the Lord that through them God will punish you, and that you will return to your vocation for all our fault finding whether you will it or not». There were two currents of opinion among the Brothers, each one of whom loved Francis, and even loved Lady Poverty, only that in her service they were ready to compromise in a way that Francis was not. Affection for Francis however won the day; for the moment the differences were passed over, the established provinces were confirmed, others were instituted, and above all it was decided to send missions to the infidels; Francis himself would lead the mission to the Mahometans in Egypt.

Missions, missions! At least in this Francis saw the growing realisation of his ideal, and the Franciscan missionary achievement was much greater than any differences within the Order. It still continues in every quarter of the globe, and the story is not yet complete.

ST. FRANCIS IN EGYPT
(1219-1221)

During Francis' absence two Vicars-General, Brothers Matthew and Gregory were appointed to «console the brothers». Accompanied by Peter Cattaneo, Illuminato and ten other brothers Francis set sail from Ancona; the longed for moment had come! Francis had been fair in his choice of companions; he would not run the risk of any selfish preference, and made a small child indicate which brothers were to go!

The group landed in Egypt where the Christian armies were besieging Damietta; Francis' first sight of them must have been coloured by his own youthful enthusiasm for chivalry and the Crusades, and by all he meant by the knighthood of the Cross. Very soon he was to find that the Christian armies were riddled with vice and corruption. No heed was given to his warnings and he was present at the defeat he had foreseen.

Meanwhile Francis had approached the Papal Legate for

Sts. Francis and Dominic meet

permission to go to the Sultan's camp and there preach Christ. The Legate must have thought him mad, for the Sultan had publicly offered a golden ducat for the head of any Christian. However he left the decision to Francis, who set out at once taking with him Brother Illuminato. They came across two lambs on the road: «Put thy trust in the Lord, Brother, said Francis gaily, for in us that saying is fulfilled: Behold I send you forth as sheep among wolves». Brother Illuminato surely rose to the occasion! They were seized by Moslem soldiers but somehow were not killed, and as Francis persistently called out «Soldan, Soldan», eventually they found themselves in the Sultan's presence, and there he preached the Gospel. Evidently Malek-el-Kamel enjoyed his unconventional visitors; perhaps he was really touched by Francis, and as a chivalrous host he ordered that the Friars should be well treated in his camp. There were several audiences, and the Soldan went so far as to invite Francis to live at his court. «Willingly», replied Francis, «if you and your people will be converted to Christ», and he went on to propose a trial by fire between himself and the priests of Mahomet, or failing them he would enter the fire alone, on condition that if he came through the Sultan should acknowledge Christ as the true God and Saviour.

Malek-el-Kamel answered that he dared not risk such a test for fear of the effect on his people, but he begged Francis to pray that he might come to know the true faith, and the guests were «conducted with courtesy» back to the Christian camp. The Sultan gave Francis an ivory and silver horn which he used henceforward to call the people together when he wished to preach. It is now among the relics of the basilica of Saint Francis in Assisi together with a hair-shirt made of camel hair which he also acquired in the East, and a little cross of box wood, a pilgrim souvenir such as we all venerate! At the Carceri hermitage there is a crucifix which he used when preaching. All these objects, with the other relics of his threadbare patched habits, bring him to life before our eyes.

Francis remained with the Crusading forces until the fall

Apparition at the Chapter of Arles

of Damietta which became a disgraceful orgy: then he left for Acre, and a number of prelates gave up their chance of preferment to enter the Fraternity. At Acre they found Brother Elias and the German friar Caesar of Speyer who had been a renowned Crusading preacher. Francis went on a preaching tour through the Christian communities of Syria; and beside this he visited the Holy Places. He left no record of that visit: how could he? And had he done so, should we have understood it? But in Bethlehem and Calvary he must have left something of himself as an undying sanctuary lamp of love.

He returned to Acre where he found Brother Stephen who had arrived from Italy bringing very bad news. Rumours were circulating there that Francis was dead, and the Order was in a state bordering on anarchy. His most faithful followers were for the most part in the hermitages, others wandered about at their own sweet will, and the Vicars had chosen to impose new regulations on the Brothers at a chapter they had held. For instance no Brother was to accept meat even on non-fasting days. Francis was at dinner when he heard this: he turned to Peter Cattaneo asking: «What are we to do?» «Father», replied Peter, «do as you think well; the decision rests with you». «Then we will eat what is set before us according to the Gospel». In the new strength and impetus accorded him in Bethlehem and Jerusalem he set out for Italy taking with him Elias and Caesar of Speyer. He went back an ill and suffering man, to face a situation of which he bore all the burden, and which he alone could remedy.

It is said that at this time he had an interview with Frederick II at the emperor's castle of Castel del Monte. Certainly in the intricate genius of Frederick there was something which responded to Francis and admired him. He is also said to have visited Monte Sant'Angelo the famous Sanctuary of Saint Michael, and tradition adds that he knelt for a whole night at the entrance holding himself unworthy to set foot in so holy a place.

ST. FRANCIS AND ST. ANTHONY
(1221-1223)

In the eighteen months or so of Francis' absence, the Vicars had done considerable mischief. Their attempts at enforcing their own ideas had confused and disunited the Brothers, some of whom had retreated into the mountain hermitages, while others wandered about. One brother John of Compello had collected a following of lepers of both sexes, and they too wished to be considered as belonging to the Fraternity.

Francis did not attempt to meet Matthew and Gregory who were responsible for at least some of the disorder, but he appealed directly to the Pope and Cardinal Ugolino. He asked that the Cardinal should be made the official Protector of the Friars, a request which Honorious at once granted, and this is a proof of Francis' trust in both Ugolino's affection and judgment in a moment of difficulty. His first act as Protector was to dismiss the two Vicars, and Peter Cattaneo became Minister General of the Fraternity, a position Francis would never accept for himself.

Francis met trouble very soon after his return, for when he arrived in Bologna he learned that the Provincial Minister for Lombardy Peter Stacia had built a convent which was certainly larger than the Friars usual dwellings. Lady Poverty was being wronged by her own knights, and with her, evangelical simplicity, for Peter was a doctor of law in the University of Bologna, and intended that the house should serve as a school for the Friars along the lines of the Dominicans. Francis refused to enter the house, indeed he lodged with the Dominicans, summoned Peter whom he accused of having wished to destroy the Fraternity, cursed him, and ordered all the Brothers to leave the convent, including those who were ill.

The question of study was a burning one for Francis, for the Friars, and for the Cardinal. Francis could not endure the idea of his Minores being trained in dialectics like the Dominicans; was it not sufficient for a Friar Minor to have

the wisdom of prayer and the learning of the Gospel?
There is a story of some French Friars who told Francis
that in Paris the brothers had appointed a learned pro-
fessor as their master. «When Francis heard this he
sighed saying: «I am afraid Brothers that such men will
end in killing my little plant. The true masters are those
who set a good example to their neighbours in good
works and kindness; for a man is learned inasmuch as he
works for others, wise inasmuch as he loves God and his
neighbour, and he is a good preacher just inasmuch as he
knows how to do good works faithfully and humbly».
It was however equally clear that some training was necessary for the Friars, as even Jacques de Vitry had seen.
Men who were not Francis or Bernard, Masseo, Leo or
Giles could not be allowed to go out and preach un-
prepared; and the Pope and Cardinal were indeed only repeating the decision of the Lateran Council when they insisted on a minimum of study. Eventually the house of
studies in Bologna was re-opened through the Cardinal's
efforts; and even Francis was not entirely against it for he
wrote to Brother Anthony, who by that time was becoming
famous as a teacher and preacher: «It pleases me that
you should read sacred theology with the Brothers so
long as this study does not extinguish the spirit of holy
prayer as is ordained in the rule». That was the crux of the
whole matter; and once and for all Francis had established the just balance between prayer and intellectual
study, a balance kept by all his greatest intellectual followers.
The Friars in Bologna received another lesson from Francis himself when he appeared there to preach in the market place on the feast of the Assumption. An eye witness
described the scene: «When I was a student in Bologna I
saw Saint Francis preach in the market place in front of
the town hall where nearly all the citizens were gathered.
He began his sermon on Angels, Men and Devils; and he
spoke so well and skillfully that many learned men who
were present were astonished to hear an unlearned man
speak thus. The whole theme of his discourse was to as-

suage enmities, and to make for peace. His habit was dirty, his appearance insignificant, his face not handsome. But God gave such power to his word that many noble families between whom there were ancient enmities and much spilled blood, allowed themselves to be induced to make peace. And all felt such devotion and reverence for him, that crowds of men and women precipitated themselves upon him, and tried to tear off bits of his habit, or even to touch the hem of his garment».

Francis himself was the irrefutable argument in favour of the principles by which he lived.

Another burning, very delicate point was that of providing the missionaries with credentials which they could produce in foreign lands as a proof of their orthodoxy. Francis, remained uncompromising: «You Friars Minor do not know the will of God, and will not allow me to convert the whole world as God wills... I wish by holy humility first to convert the prelates; and when they see our holy life and our humble reverence towards them, they will themselves ask you to preach and convert the people: and they will summon the people to hear you preaching better than your privileges which will only lead you to pride... For myself I wish only this privilege from the Lord that I may never have any privilege from man, save only the privilege to do reverence to all and to convert mankind through obedience to our holy rule, more than by word». If awful things happened to the missionaries Francis could only say: «Wherever they are not received, let them flee into another land to live in penance with the blessing of God».

Notwithstanding this, the Pope and the Cardinal were agreed in insisting that the missionaries must be protected by carrying credentials from the Holy See. The missions themselves were too important to be jeopardized.

There is no doubt that the Cardinal tried to respect Francis' wishes to the utmost, even when he did not agree with them. Francis heard only the voice of Christ in his own vocation: the Cardinal saw the unavoidable human results. He was passionately anxious to preserve and help the growing plant of Francis' work, and yet there was

Choir at San Damiano

bound to be a change between the developing plant and the seedling.

The Cardinal favoured a more definite organisation of the Fraternity, and this was becoming inevitable owing to the numbers of men who wished to join it, many of whom were probably attracted by the general enthusiasm evoked by Francis, and had not passed through any deep personal spiritual experience such as that of the First Companions. At first there had been no novitiate, and Francis trusted to his own sure instinct in choosing his brothers; but by this time he could not possibly know each friar personally, and a novitiate was essential. Hitherto the brothers had lived in the smallest and most humble of dwellings for Francis held that Lady Poverty could only be loyally served where the Friars were few. Many of these «places» were hermitages such as a La Verna, the Carceri, Greccio, Le Celle and others, and from the beginning,the Franciscan vocation included the hermit life of contemplation. Francis himself continually fled to the hills to replenish the lamp of his own spiritual life through prayer and solitude which were as necessary to him as light and air. He gave his contemplative brothers a very simple form of life; after his death the contemplative and active currents in the Order tended to separate and become more crystallised, and the balance so delicately held by Francis was lost.

At the time of which we are speaking however there was little provision for the common life of the ever increasing number of Brothers; and the first step in organisation was made by Honorious III, probably at the Cardinal's instigation, when he decreed a year's novitiate, and that once professed, no friar could pass into another order; and that no one might wander about the country without letters of obedience from his Guardian.

During Francis' absence the Cardinal had also turned his attention to San Damiano for there too the question of organisation had arisen. Clare and her sisters had lived hitherto according to the simple form of life given them by Francis; but when they became a recognized religious order this no longer sufficed. Cardinal Ugolino drew up the «rule» for San Damiano, and the result pleased neither Francis nor Clare: nevertheless she and her sisters observed it loyally for thirty years! She wished for one thing: the sanction for complete poverty, and in the very end she won after a long and arduous tussle. She and Francis worked as hard for poverty as many folk do for riches.

At this time the Cardinal also drew up a rule for Francis' outer circle of followers: it was based on that given by Innocent III to the Umiliati. We only know it in a later version, but through the formal phrases it is possible to catch the spirit of Francis, as most certainly those followers did, and proved it in their lives.

Meanwhile the Brothers from every province were summoned to attend the general Chapter at the Porziuncula at Pentecost of 1221. Three thousand came and how they must have questioned Elias and Caesar about Francis' journey in the east! Probably the first bit of news was that of the martyrdom of the five missionaries to Morocco. «Now I have five real Brothers», Francis exclaimed, and all knew how willingly he would have been in their place! «Let each man glory in his own martyrdom, not in that of others». That was what Francis felt.

Incidentally it was the martyrdom of those Brothers which brought the young Portuguese canon, the future Saint Anthony of Padua into the Franciscan Order.

Peter Cattaneo had recently died, and been succeeded by the forceful Brother Elias, a man of two distinct sides, one of which was that of a genius, and he genuinely loved Francis. The Cardinal was not present, and Francis met the Brothers with the determination to reassert his own original vocation. The primitive ideal was kept intact, and several points were emphasized that sounded the primitive note. For instance the Brothers were forbidden to meddle in temporal affairs, manual labour was again stressed, and it was also said the Brothers were «to bear themselves merrily and joyfully and always be becomingly gracious». The Gospel liberty in regard to food was maintained, and it was stated that no Brother was bound to obey a Minister if he should order anything manifestly contrary to the Franciscan vocation. What was more the Brothers could admonish any Minister whom they saw «walking according to the flesh and not according to the spirit», and such a Minister could be reported to a General Chapter.

One Minister asked Francis what was really meant by the clause in the rule that said that travelling Brothers should carry nothing with them. Francis replied that it meant exactly what is said. «What then shall I do with my books"» asked the Minister. «Brother, I cannot go against my conscience and the profession of the holy Gospel we have promised to observe... O you Brothers who wish to be called Friars Minor, and to appear to people as observers of the Gospel, and yet in fact want your treasure chests! But I am not going to lose the book of the Gospel for the sake of your books. Do what you will, but my permission shall never be made a snare to the Brothers».

The chapter had already lasted a week, and Francis was so exhausted that he sat on the ground at Elias' feet, and pulled him by the habit whenever he wished to speak. No wonder his strength gave out, for his health was broken, and his eyes were dim with trachoma. The robust Elias acted as a megaphone, prefacing any declaration with «the Brother says»; there was only one «The Brother» in the Fraternity. On this occasion Francis wished to draw the Chapter's attention to the fact that no further provision had been made for new missions to Germany. The fate of the former mission had not been encouraging, but at once «ninety Brothers rose, offering themselves to death». Giordano di Giano tells us that he took pains to speak to each of these brothers on the chance that in the future he might be able to boast of having talked to a martyr! Twenty five started under the leadership of Caesar of Speyer; and this time the effort was successful. Among other enthusiasts for the Franciscan ideal it brought the future Saint Elizabeth of Hungary, the patroness of the Order of Penance, into touch with Francis. The fame of her sanctity quickly reached him, and he sent her his old cloak which she used to put round her when praying.

Again the Order had found its deep unity in the missions. The great excitement among all the Brothers however was Francis' own return, for the rumours of his death in Syria had disturbed many. Now he was back, he was the same as ever, and all the old enthusiasm and loyally revived among his friends. He was indeed the same, and no matter how perturbed he might be over the affairs of the Fraternity, as he was walking through some marshes he noticed a multitude of birds singing. «Whereupon he said to the Brother who was with him: «Our sisters are praising their Creator; let us go among them and chant our hours», and the birds continued unalarmed. Finding however that after a time their voices distracted him, Francis bade them be quiet until he had fulfilled his debt to the Lord. Then, the Office finished, he gave them a sign, and they again began to sing».

Such episodes must have come to him at that time like rays of sun in which he could escape from the human difficulties into the universal song of praise of God's whole creation.

There must also have been human consolations, for Giordano di Giano looking back later on these very days could say of them: «Who can express the charity, patience, humility, obedience, and fraternal merriment there was among the Brothers». For many of the Brothers their vocation was still a glorious adventure of faith, and trust, and divine inspiration; especially with Francis in their midst, and this too must have sustained him who so desired unity and peace for his Fraternity and saw it being chipped and cracked by difference of opinion and divergencies in loyalty.

He was increasingly hemmed in and oppressed by anxiety over the Fraternity: «Would there were fewer Friars Minor» he was heard to exclaim «and that seeing a Friar Minor rarely, the world should wonder at their fewness». At the Porziuncula he was seen weeping bitterly and imploring God's mercy on himself and his brothers; his spiritual and physical suffering grew with each, as it seemed to him, new slight to Lady Poverty, each betrayal of the divine vocation of the Gospel. Had he chosen to assert himself, as the leader of those brothers who felt as he did, there is no doubt a number would have followed him; but he would not provoke a schism in the Fraternity; his protest was to live the rule as he had always done, «simple and subject to all». It was not only the Franciscan vocation that was being tried and forged in the fire, but Francis himself. Clare was one those who were spiritually closest to him during this tremendous trial, and we catch an eloquent glimpse of him at San Damiano in the spring of 1223.

He spoke to no one, and went straight to the chapel, and stood there for some time, silent with uplifted arms beneath the crucifix which had once spoken to him. At last he turned and asked for ashes, and when they were brought he sprinkled them on his own head, and all round him on the ground. Then he intoned the Miserere after which he left hastily, and in silence.

This visit was part of Francis' preparation for the Pentecost chapter; and his own spiritual struggle is expressed in the words recorded by his friends. Even Francis felt some temptation to domination «If I come to the chapter I will show them of what kind my will is». It was a natural instinct; but he knew to that nothing would be gained along those lines, and he continued, as one talking to himself: «Behold the brothers, with great devotion invite me to the chapter... and when gathered there they beseech me to announce the word of God, and rising up I preach to them as the Holy Spirit shall have taught me.

Suppose that when I end, all cry out aginst me: «We will not have you to govern us for you have not the suitable eloquence, and you are too simple and unlearned; and we should be sorely ashamed to have so simple and despised a superior; therefore do not presume to govern us. And so they cast me out in contempt and disgrace. It seems to me that I am no Friar Minor if I do not rejoice when they hold me as being of no account and cast me out with shame». He was putting into practice his parable of «Perfect Joy».

He also wrote a most symptomatic letter to Brother Elias, the Minister General: «I will tell thee my ideas as well as I can; that thou should'st regard it only as blessing when the Brothers and other men oppose thee, Thou must wish that it should be so, and not otherwise... I know with certainty that this is true obedience. Love those who are opposed to thee, and wish nothing else for them than what the Lord shall give thee. And herein show thy charity that thou shalt not wish them to be better Christians; and that for thee shall be more than to withdraw to a hermitage».

Francis had the right to preach to Elias, for at infinite cost he had learnt the lessons that he taught.

The question of another and final revision of the rule was again discussed at the chapter; and it was becoming increasingly urgent that there should be a clarification in its wording, and that it should be endorsed by the final and definite approval of the Holy See.

Francis taking with him Brothers Bonizzo, and Leo his secretary, retired to a hermitage in the mountains above Rieti to compose this rule, «and what the Lord revealed to him in prayer, he told those brothers»... «Now there was great commotion among the brothers in Italy because they knew that Francis was composing this new rule, and one minister excited the next. They went to Brother Elias saying: «We have heard that Brother Francis is writing a new rule, and we are afraid that it will be too hard to be followed. For he is very strict with himself, and could easily command us things we cannot observe. Say this to him therefore before it is ratified by the Pope».

Elias refused to go alone to Francis so they all went together. When they came near the place, Brother Elias called, «The Lord be praised». Then Francis appeared, and asked Elias: «What do these Brothers want? Did I not say that no one was to come here?».

Brother Elias answered: «The Ministers of Italy are here, for they have heard that thou writest a new rule, therefore they say thou shalt write it so that they can obey it; if not they will not bind themselves by it, and thou canst write it for thyself, and not for them».

Francis could only reply that the rule was dictated to him by Christ, and this he always claimed.

This rule appears to have been lost, and Francis, who had delivered it to Elias at the Porziuncula, returned to the hermitage on Monte Rainerio to rewrite it. Again the Ministers pursued him, protesting that they could not observe it; he could only repeat that they had best leave the Fraternity. Anyhow the rule which has led thousands to the heights of sanctity was re-written, and Francis himself

Christmas at Greccio (1223)

went to Rome and presented it to Honorious III who solemnly approved it on November 29th 1223.

Even then he was harassed by complaints, but perhaps it was about this time that he was also comforted by a vision of Our Lord Who spoke to him: «O little Poor Man, why are you distressed? Have I set you as a shepherd over My religion, and you do not know that I am its chief Protector? I set you over it, a simple man, to the end that those who will, may follow you in those things I work in you for an example to others. It is I who have called them; I who will keep and feed them; and I will make good the falling away of some by putting others in their place, and if these be not born, I will cause them to be born. Be not therefore perturbed, but work out thy salvation; for even if the religion should come only to three members, yet through My gift it shall remain unshaken».

«Be not perturbed: work out thy salvation». Without knowing it Francis had reached another milestone and was setting out for the final experiences of his life which were to complete the work of his santification.

ST. FRANCIS AT GRECCIO
(1223-1226)

After the suffering, the struggles and darkness of the rule difficulties, Francis turned to Our Lord with a new self dedication, an increase of love, and faith, and his mind may easily have reverted to Bethlehem and Calvary. It was Advent, and before leaving Rome he asked the Pope's permission to represent outwardly the poverty of Christ in the manger. He may have remembered Nativity dramas seen during his childhood in which the crib, that is a representation of the manger, was the centre of the play; such plays had fallen into disrepute and had indeed been forbidden, which explains the reason for Francis' request.

Shortly before Christmas he was back on Monte Rainerio and sent for a friend Giovanni Vellita, and told him to prepare for the feast in the hermitage of Greccio, which was

Hermitage of the Carceri

another of Francis' favourite mountain retreats. «I desire to represent the birth of that Child in Bethlehem in such a way that with our bodily eyes we may see all that He suffered for lack of the necessities for a new-born babe, and how He lay in the manger between the ox and ass». For Francis Christmas had always been the «feast of feasts», the feast of light and hope, of peace and joy and brotherly love, the day when «Heaven and earth are made one», when God «condescended to be fed by human love». He would have liked to see every poor man handsomely entertained, and every ox and ass treated to double rations, and corn scattered for the birds. Christmas was the feast of Lady Poverty, and when at dinner a brother spoke of the poverty suffered by Christ and His Mother in Bethlehem, Francis, weeping for compassion, would no longer sit at the table, but finished his food crouching on the floor. He wanted, not to preach a sermon on poverty, but to illustrate once again for himself and for every brother what was the poverty of Christ.

Giovanni willingly fell in with Francis' plan and arranged a manger filled with hay, and sent an invitation to all the friars and people of the neighbourhood; and many brothers and good people came to Greccio during that night when the weather also was most beautiful. A great quantity of lights had been kindled, many songs and hymns were sung with great solemnity by the many brothers, so that all the wood echoed with the sound, and the man of God stood before the manger filled with the utmost joy, and shedding tears of devotion and compassion. By his order the manger had been so arranged that Mass was celebrated on it, and blessed Francis, the Levite of Christ, sang the Gospel, and preached to the people on the Nativity of Christ our King, and when he pronounced His Name with infinite tenderness and love, he called Him «the little Babe of Bethlehem». Saint Bonaventure goes on to tell of the vision of Giovanni who saw a seemingly lifeless child in the manger until Francis approached and woke him, «nor was this vision untrue, for by the grace of God, through His servant Blessed Francis, Christ was

Miracle of the Spring

awakened in many hearts where formerly He slept»...
«Greccio was transformed almost into a second Bethlehem and that wonderful night seemed like the fullest day to both man and beast for the joy they felt at the renewing of the mystery».

Francis had succeeded in his wish that this particular Christmas celebration should «move the people to greater devotion»; he had given new life to the crib of the Nativity plays, and his inspiration is still alive in every Christmas Crib in every church and home.

Francis' joy that Christmas expressed itself in a canticle which he composed for the whole octave and which he may quite well have sung in the woods as well as in the chapel of Greccio.

«Rejoice to God our Helper; shout unto God living and
[true with the voice of triumph.

For the Lord is high, terrible, a great King over all the earth.

For the most holy Father of Heaven our everlasting King
[sent His beloved Son From on high

And He was born of the Blessed Virgin, holy Mary.

He shall cry to Me, «Thou art my Father», and I will make
[Him My First-born,

High over the kings of the earth.

In the day-time the Lord has commanded His mercy; and
[a canticle to Him in the night.

This is the day wich the Lord has made; let us rejoice
[and be glad in it.

For the beloved and most holy Child has been given us,
[born for us by the wayside,

And laid in a manger because he had no room in the inn.

Glory to God in the highest, and on earth peace to men
[of good will.

Let the heavens rejoice and the earth be glad; let the sea
[be moved and the fullness of it.

The fields shall rejoice and all that is in them.

Sing to the Lord a new canticle; sing to the Lord all
[the earth.

For the Lord is great and exceedingly to be praised; He is
[to be feared above all the gods.

Bring to the Lord O ye kindreds of the Gentiles, bring to
[the Lord glory and honour.
Bring to the Lord glory unto His name. Bring your own
[bodies and bear His holy cross;
And follow His most holy precepts unto the end».

Francis stayed on at Greccio with a hare as his close companion and friend. It was perhaps during that Lent that he composed the Office of the Passion for Clare who, like him, lived in the Passion as an ever present, and ever happening reality. She recited this Office every day.

On Easter Sunday he gave the brothers another improvised demonstration of poverty. He had found the dinner table set with some slight show of what he considered luxury; when the brothers were assembled he knocked at the door with a beggar's hat on, and a staff in his hand. «For the love of the Lord give alms to this poor sick pilgrim». They called to him to enter, and Francis accepted his portion of food and ate it sitting on the ground. «Now I am seated like a Friar Minor. When I saw the table so well set and adorned it seemed to me not the table of men who beg their bread from door to door. More than all other religious we should be constrained to follow the poverty of Christ, the Son of God».

Again that year he attended the Pentecost chapter at which all the brothers must have professed the revised rule. Francis spoke to the assembly and he also wrote a letter emphasizing those points which were to him so essential, such as the devotion to the Blessed Sacrament, and the injunction that the Office was to be recited with more attention to inner devotion than to the manner of singing. He insisted anew on the care due to churches, and that the Blessed Sacrament must be preserved with the utmost reverence; and that when the host is consecrated during Mass the church bells are to be rung so that all within earshot can participate in the giving of praise to God. «And I Brother Francis, you little servant, pray and beseech you in charity which is God Himself, and with the desire to kiss your feet, that you should accept these and others of the words of Our Lord Jesus

Christ, and should practise them and keep them perfectly in humility and charity... And who does not do this shall be called to account at the last day before the judgment seat of Christ. And those who accept these words joyfully, and embrace them, and are an example to others, if they persevere in living thus to the end, may they be blessed by God the Father, the Son and the Holy Ghost, Amen».

The most important decision of the chapter was to establish a province of the Friars Minor in England; and the mission set out led by Brother Albert of Pisa.

After the chapter Francis started towards the hermitage of La Verna accompained by Leo, Masseo, Angelo, Illuminato, Sylvester and Bonizzo, all tried and intimate friends. His object was to keep the Lent of Saint Michael in the mountain hermitage, for all mountains were sacred to the Archangel, and Francis' great devotion to the Angels, our defenders against the powers of evil, expressed itself in this fast of six weeks ending on September 29th the feast of Saint Michael.

This time Francis could not manage the journey on foot: and at one stage he was so suffering that his companions persuaded a passing peasant to lend his ass. The peasant erguired «Art thou that Brother Francis of whom so much is said?». When Francis assented the peasant continued: «then take care thou art as good as they say, for many trust in thee». Francis slipped on to his knees to kiss the man's feet and thank him for the warning. It may have been for this same peasant that later on when they had no water, a spring gushed out of the rock at Francis' prayer. Everything on the mountain of Alvernia spoke to Francis of Christ's Passion; and one day while he was wondering at the sudden deep chasms and fissures in the abrupt, piled up rocks, it was revealed to him that the extraordinary conformation of the hill had been «miraculously wrought in the hour of Christ's passion when as the evangelist says: «the rocks were rent asunder». Was it any wonder that Francis should exclaim: «weep hills, weep mountains, rocks rend yourselves; valleys heave deep sighs. because Love is not loved».

Stigmatization of Franci

All his friends testify, to his constant preoccupation with the mystery of the Passion. Ever since his first vision of Christ crucified, «his heart was so sore and melted with the memory of Christ's sufferings that all his life he bore the wounds of Jesus in his heart». His early experience in San Damiano had never been dimmed, «and from that hour he was pierced with compassion for the crucified Saviour, so that for the rest of his life he bore in his heart the holy wounds which later were impressed upon his body. The sufferings of Christ were ever before his eyes, and filled them with ever-flowing tears». Body and soul he belonged to Christ crucified; the words he had written at Greccio, «bring your own bodies and bear His holy cross» expressed his own deep longing for martyrdom; he could not then know how soon they were to become a reality.

At Alvernia he had a little cell made, somewhat apart from the cells of the other brothers. He wished for complete solitude, and only Leo his confessor and secretary was to come at stated times and bring him food; and even Leo was to announce his presence by calling out on the far side of a plank bridge, the opening verse of Matins. If Francis answered, Leo could cross the plank, if not, he was to turn away.

A falcon became Francis' inseparable companion and was entrusted with the task of waking him for Matins if he overslept, «and for that falcon he had a great love».

Leo was the witness of his master's alternations of mood. Sometimes he was preoccupied with the brothers, «Lord I commit to Thee the family Thou hast given me I cannot lead them any longer myself». Then comfort came with a vision of Christ, or as on another occasion with wonderful music played for him by an angel. Suffering however was the dominant note, and Francis told him: «If the brothers did but know how grievous are the afflictions and anguish which the devils work on me, there is not one who would not be moved with pity and tenderness towards me». On one occasion the rock opened to save him from being hurled over a precipice.

One night when Leo came there was no answer to the

Francis' autographed blessing for Brother Leo

usual signal; but still he crossed the plank and found Francis kneeling in the moonlit wood with uplifted face and arms, and fervently repeating: «Who art Thou my most sweet God, and who am I Thy most useless servant?» Leo saw a flame descend on to Francis' head and three times he reached up towards it with his hand, until finally the flame disappeared. Later Francis told him that Christ had asked of him three gifts, and bidden him to take them from his own heart. Inside his tunic Francis had found three golden balls which he then understood represented poverty, chastity and obedience. After this they went to the chapel where Leo said Mass and Francis threw himself on the ground praying that he might be shown the intentions of God. As in old days he bade Leo open the Gospels thrice, and each time Leo's eye fell on a passage from the Passion. It may well have been the feast of the Exaltation of the Cross when every word of the Liturgy struck home into the depths of Francis' heart and prayed: «Lord Jesus Christ I beg of Thee two favours before I die. The first is that as far as is possible I may feel in my soul and body the suffering which Thou endured in Thy bitter Passion. And the second is that I may receive into my heart that exceeding love by which Thou, the Son of God, wast inflamed, and which moved Thee willingly to suffer so much for us sinners.

And as he prayed thus, he felt the certainty that God would grant him these two things... and after he had received this promise, he began with great devotion to meditate on the sufferings of Christ and on his boundless charity, and the glow of piety grew so strong in him, that through charity and pity he was all transformed in Jesus».
The Fioretti continue with details that must have been supplied by Francis to his companions and recorded by them: «As he lay in this prayer and burned with this flame, behold in the same morning hour he saw a seraph coming slowly from Heaven having six luminous wings. And the seraph slowly approached Francis so that he could clearly see and discern that it bore the image of a crucified man, and its wings were so disposed that two were raised

above its head, two extended for flying, and two covered its body.

When Francis saw this vision he was greatly afraid, and at the same time filled with joy and sorrow and wonder. He had great joy at the sight of Jesus Who showed Himself so intimately and looked at him with such love, but it gave him inexpressible sorrow to see the Lord fastened to the cross; moreover he wondered over so unusual and astonishing a vision for he knew that mortal suffering is not compatible with a seraph's immortal spirit. While he thus wondered Christ revealed to him that God granted him this vision that he should understand that not by bodily martyrdom, but by an inner flame he was to be entirely tranformed into the likeness of Christ crucified. After the wonderful vision had finally departed an excessive glow was left in Francis' heart with a living love of God, and in his body the seraph left a wonderful image of Christ's sufferings, At once in his hands and feet marks like nails began to appear, so that they seemed perforated, and the heads of the nails were in the palms of the hands, and on the upper side of the feet, and the points of the nails were in the backs of the hands and soles of the feet... and in his left side the image of a lance thrust appeared, red and bleeding and the blood often saturated Francis' habit».

A corner of the cloud over Calvary will always veil Alvernia, and Francis teaches us that only love can partially lift it.

That night the glow on the mountain was so bright that some muleteers got up and saddled their mules to start on their journey to Romagna for they thought that the day had come.

As always distrustful of his own self-will, Francis called his brothers and asked them whether he should speak or be silent about a favour God had granted him. Illuminato answered: «Brother thou knowest that the heavenly secrets are revealed to thee not only for thyself, but also for others». Then Francis told them, and broke into one of his beautiful songs which has been called his Praise of the Lord.

«Thou art the holy Lord God; Thou art God of gods Who
[only workest marvels.
Thou art strong; Thou art great; Thou art great; Thou art
most high;   [thou art almighty.
Thou holy Father, King of heaven and earth.
Thou art threefold and one; Lord God of gods.
Thou art good, every good, the highest good; the Lord
[God living and true.
Thou art love, Thou art charity; Thou art wisdom; Thou
[art humility;
Thou art patience, fortitude and prudence;
Thou art security, Thou art rest; Thou art joy and glad-
ness.
Thou art justice and temperance; Thou art all our wealth
[and plenty.
Thou art beauty, Thou art gentleness; Thou art the
[protector,
Thou art the keeper and defender.
Thou art our refuge and strength; Thou art our faith, hope
and charity.
Thou art our great sweetness; Thou art our eternal life.

Infinite Goodness, great and wonderful Lord God almighty,   [loving and merciful Saviour».
He had experienced every word he sang and wrote; and if
possible it brought him nearer to his fellow men than before. He knew that Leo his huge friend whom be had nicknamed «Little lamb of God» was feeling despairing, lonely
and left behind, and that of himself he could not break the
ice. So he turned over the parchment on which the Praises
were written, and wrote on the reverse: **«The Lord bless
thee and keep thee. The Lord show his face to thee and
have mercy upon thee. The Lord turn His countenance to
thee and give thee peace. «Brother Leo may Our Lord
bless thee».** Beneath the words he drew the sign of the
Thau so that it passed through the letters of Leo's name.
He handed it to him saying: «Take this and carefully keep
it till thy death». Leo confirmed the authenticity of the parchment annotating it in red ink in his small, neat writing,

The canticle of the creatures

Most high onnipotent good Lord,
  to Thee Praise, glory, honour,
  and every benediction.
To Thee alone Most High do they belong.
  And no man is worthy to pronounce Thy Name.
Praise be to Thee my Lord with all Thy creatures.
  Especially for Master Brother Sun
  Who illuminates the day for us,
  And Thee Most High he manifests.
Praise be to Thee my Lord
  for Sister Moon and for the stars.
  In Heaven Thou hast formed them,
  shining, precious, fair.
Praise be to Thee my Lord for Brother Wind,
  For air and clouds,
  clear sky and all the weathers
  Through which Thou sustainest all Thy creatures.
Praise be to Thee my Lord for Sister Water.
  She is useful and humble, precious and pure.
Praise be to Thee my Lord for Brother Fire,
  Through him our night Thou dost enlighten,
  And he is fair and merry, boisterous and strong.
Praise be to Thee my Lord for our sister Mother
  Earth,
  Who nourishes and sustains us all,
  Bringing forth divers fruits,
  and many-coloured flowers and herbs.
Praise be to Thee my Lord for those
  who pardon grant for love of Thee
  And bear infirmity and tribulation,
  Blessed be those who live in peace,
  For by Thee Most High they shall be crowned.
Praise be to Thee my Lord

  for our Sister Bodily Death
  From whom no living man can flee;
  Woe to them who die in mortal sin
  But blessed they who shall be found
  in Thy most holy Will;
  To them the second death can do no harm.
O bless and praise my Lord all creatures,
  And thank and serve Him in deep humility.

ST. FRANCIS

and he left it to the Church of Saint Francis in Assisi, where it is preserved.

Before leaving Alvernia Francis bade Ruffino consecrate the stone on which the seraphs wing had rested and commanded the brothers always to hold it in the highest honour. For more than seven hundred years twice every day Francis' sons have gone, and go, in procession to what is now the chapel of the Stigmata, and with outstretched arms repeat, «Signasti Domine hic servum Tuum Franciscum, signis redemptionis nostrae», after which there is silence, and then they take up the chanting of a psalm of praise. It is said that on the rare occasions when storms have beaten the friars, animals have taken their place, leaving the trace of their feet in the snow. Francis took a most loving and courteous leave of his brothers and his mountain commending them all to God: «peace be with you dearest sons, farewell. I go from you in the body, but I leave my heart with you. Farewell holy mountain; mount Alvernia, Mount of angels! Farewell dearest Brother Falcon; I thank thee for thy love! Farewell Sasso Spicco... we shall never see each other again. To thee Mother of the eternal Word, to thee I commend my sons».

The journey back to the Porziuncula was made by slow stages: Francis could not walk; and often he was so lost in prayer that he did not even notice the places through which they passed; wherever they stopped he healed the sick. Leo saw a luminous cross preceding them on the way, and on the cross was the figure of Christ.

Francis seems to have chosen this moment for a final act of selfdenial in depriving himself of his intimate friends, and especially of Brother Leo, who, since the Stigmata, had redoubled his care. Perhaps other brothers, a little more human in their reactions grumbled; perhaps they felt possessive and jealous that anyone should do more for Francis than they, and he sensed the tension and said to the Minister General: «I do not wish for the singular privilege of having a special companion. I want to associate equally with all the brothers in each place as God may inspire them to desire»... Not long ago I saw a blind man led little dog: I do not want to appear more important than him». It was an act of tremendous homage to Lady Poverty for Francis to part with Brother Leo who so well understood his spiritual and physical needs; perhaps the other brothers realized that his departure was a mistake, and we find Francis writing to him in such a manner as to show that the way was open for his return: «Brother Leo, wish thy brother Francis health and peace. I say to thee; yes my son, and as a mother; and in this word and advice I sum up briefly all the words we said on the way; and if afterwards thou has need to come to me for counsel, thus I advise thee. In whatever way it seemeth best to thee to please the Lord God, and to follow His footsteps and poverty, so do with the blessing of the Lord God and in my obedience. And if it be necessary for thee on account of thy soul, or other consolation, and thou wishest, Leo, to come to me, then come».

Incredible as it seems Francis had not been long at the Porziuncula when he wished to start off on another preaching tour. He was almost blind, he could not walk, he was a desperately sick man, but he started. The first halt was at San Damiano where Clare had a hut built for him in the garden: probably she never knew that it was overrun with mice. San Damiano had never failed Francis, and Clare had never failed him; and especially after the Stigmata he must have wished to kneel again before his crucifix and to feel himself surrounded with the praise and prayer of the sisters.

One night he was especially suffering and besought God's help. Then he heard a question: «Tell me Brother, if in return for thy suffering thou should'st be promised a treasure so vast and precious that by comparison the whole earth would be as nothing, would'st thou not greatly rejoice?

«Great indeed O Lord would be this treasure, and very precious, and exceedingly wonderful and desirable».

«Then Brother be glad and make merry in thy infirmities; and for the rest be assured of My kingdom, even as though thou wert already there».

When morning came the brothers found him radiant: «The Lord has deigned to assure me, His unworthy servant of the possession of His kingdom even while I still live in the flesh. Wherefore to the praise of the Lord, and for our own comfort and for the edification of our neighbour, I will make a new hymn concerning those creatures of the Lord which minister to our daily need and without which we could not live:

«Most high omnipotent good Lord, to Thee be
Praise, glory, honour and every benediction.
To Thee alone Most High do they belong,
And no man is worthy to pronounce Thy Name.
Praise be to Thee my Lord with all Thy creatures,
Especially our Master Brother sun
Who illuminates the day for us,
And he is beautiful, and radiant and resplendent,
And Thee most High, he manifests.
Praise be to Thee my Lord for Sister Moon and for the stars
In heaven Thou hast formed them shining, precious, fair.
Praise be to Thee my Lord for Brother Wind
For air and clouds, clear sky and all the weathers
Through which Thou sustainest all Thy creatures.
Praise be to Thee my Lord for Sister Water,
She is useful and humble, precious and pure.
Praise be to Thee my Lord for Brother Fire,
Through him our night Thou dost enlighten,
And he is fair and merry, boisterous and strong.
Praise be to Thee my Lord for our sister Mother Earth,
Who nourishes and sustains us all,
Bringing forth divers fruits and many-coloured flowers and herbs.

O bless and praise my Lord all creatures,
And thank and serve Him in deep humility.
For Francis humility was the keynote in all praise as in love: this canticle was his grace for the whole of creation, and he had lived it each day of his life; it was his answer to all the sufferings, trials, disappointments. He was delighted with his song, and had it set to music by Brother

Pacifico: indeed he wished that it should be sung after every sermon, and then the preacher could say: «We are the Lord's minstrels, and we wish you to pay us for this service by abiding in penitence».

Francis had praised God for the elements His creatures, but there was still something lacking in the Canticle. How should he sing of man? Not man in his sinful separation from God, but in his wholeness, of whom it could be said that Christ «lives in him». While Francis was at San Damiano, in Assisi a quarrel flared up between the Bishop and the Podestà. They appealed to him and he appointed a day for them to meet. No doubt they expected he would be there, but he would not set himself up as an arbitrator. Instead he sent a group of friars to sing the Canticle with a new stanza composed for the occasion:

«Praise be to Thee my Lord for those who grant pardon
[for love of Thee,
And bear infirmity and tribulation,
Blessed be those who live in peace,
For by Thee most High they shall be crowned».

He had found the point at which man is nearest to Christ, and therefore worthy to enter into the universal song of praise. Perhaps those who listened knew of the dissensions within the Fraternity, some may have guessed what they meant to Francis. However that may have been, the words went home, and the Bishop and Podestà were reconciled.

At last the day came when Clare and the sisters had to let him go, and he may still have dreamed of a missionary journey, but his immediate destination was Rieti where Cardinal Ugolino wished him to consult an oculist. The journey was a triumphal progress; the news of the stigmata had flown through the countryside and everybody wanted to see him. Already it had been said of Francis that he was not so much a man who prayed as an impersonation of prayer; so too there was no further need for him to preach, since he had become a living sermon, and those who approached him dared to call him an «alter Christus». At La Foresta where he was lodged with the parish priest the people stampeded through the vineyards helping themselves liberally to the priest's ripe grapes. «Do not worry» said Francis to the disconsolate priest, «we can do nothing now, but we can trust in the Lord to repay you for the loss you have suffered through me, tell me how many measures of wine do you count on in a good year?» «Twelve», replied the priest. Francis promised him twenty, and a few days later when the vintage was finished, twenty full measures came from the press.

Wherever he passed he was accessible to all who sought him, and many sick folk were healed. In one place he found a leper whom no one could please and who abused those who cared for him «with word and blow, and continually reviled God and the saints».

«God give thee peace dear Brother», was Francis' greeting, to which the wretched leper replied: «What peace can I have when God has taken everything from me, and has made me all decayed and malodorous? I would not even complain of my disease but the Brothers whom thou hast set to wait on me do not care for me as they should». Then Francis said: «Son, since the others do not content thee, shall I wait on thee?» «I should like that», answered the leper, «but what couldst thou do for me more than the others?» «I will do all thou wishest», said Francis; whereupon the leper replied: «Then I want thee to wash me all over for the odour is such that I cannot stand it».

Then Saint Francis had warm water prepared with many aromatic herbs; he undressed the sick man and began to wash him with his own hands, and another Brother helped. And by a miracle from God it happened that where Saint Francis touched him with his blessed hands the leprosy disappeared and the flesh became entirely healed. And when the leper saw that he was cured, he was overcome with great grief and emotion because of his sins and began to weep bitterly. And when he was entirely healed in soul and body, he began in humility to accuse himself and weeping in a loud voice: «Woe to me who have made myself worthy of hell by the injustice I have

St. Francis' Tomb

done the Brothers, and by my impatience and blasphemy».

And Saint Francis thanked God for so great a miracle, and went away to distant places for in his humility he wished to flee from all honour, and sought in all things only God's honour and glory and not his own».

By this time Francis was never out of pain, and one day when he was suffering more than usual he asked a Brother who was a skilled musician to borrow a violin «and bring comfort to Brother Body who is so full of pain». The Brother demurred, fearing scandal. «In that case» added Francis, «let it be. It is better to put aside even good things rather than to scandalize others». That night however he told how he had heard wonderful music, far sweeter than that of any earthly instrument.

The Rieti oculist wished to cauterize his temples, and for a moment Francis seems to have been afraid of flinching. Then he looked at the iron heating in the brazier: «O my brother Fire, amongst all creatures most noble and useful, be courteous to me in this hour, for I have ever loved thee for love of Him Who created thee». He said that he felt no pain during the operation; it was useless and gave him no relief; neither did the opening of the veins above his ears, and a further cauterisation of the ears.

He still talked of returning to the service of the lepers: «my Brothers let us begin to serve the Lord God for hitherto we have done nothing, or hardly anything». The old missionary impulse surged up in him, and he also talked of the life of prayer in the hermitages. He wrote a letter to the governors and magistrates in all parts of the world begging them to see that due reverence was paid to the Blessed Sacrament, and that the town crier every morning and in every place should call upon people to praise God. He wrote another letter in the same vein to all the Custodes of the Fraternity.

Cardinal Ugolino wished him to consult other doctors in Siena, and he submitted himself completely to Ugolino and Brother Elias who certainly surrounded Francis with every care he could think of. On the way to Siena in the

Francis blesses Assisi

undulating country round San Quirico the party was met by three poor women, alike in features and dress. They bowed to Francis and greeted him with the words: «Welcome Sir Poverty». Then they passed on. Francis bade one of his companions to run after them with an alms, but they had disappeared. The story went that they were the three evangelical virtues, for Francis they were heavenly witnesses to his marriage with Lady Poverty.

In Siena he was received with the greatest affection and reverence, and someone gave him a pheasant as a companion. But the doctors proved equally helpless and one day he had a violent haemorrhage which terrified the Brothers. He dictated a letter meant for all the brothers which ended «in token of my memory and blessing and last will they are to love another as I have loved them; for ever to love and observe our Lady Poverty and always to be loyal subjects to the prelates and clergy of Holy Mother Church».

Meanwhile Elias had been sent for and hurried to Siena in order to take Francis back to Assisi. It was his own wish, for Francis loved his Assisi and the Porziuncola with truly Italian devotion: by this time too his fellow citizens well knew that he was their greatest treasure, and in an age of excessive relic-hunting they would never have forgiven Elias had Francis not reached his home to die.

The journey back took them by way of the Celle hermitage at Cortona; then, avoiding Perugia for fear of an attempt to kidnap Francis, they took the road leading by Gubbio and Nocera where an armed escort from Assisi met them. At Satriano the villagers would not sell the soldiers any food, and Francis pointed out that this was the result of trusting in «flies» as he called money, instead of in God. He told the guards to go back and humbly beg in the name of God, upon which the villagers relented.

All Assisi came out to meet Francis, and he was lodged in the house of his old friend Bishop Guido. Ministers and Brothers from all over Italy gathered at Saint Mary of the Angels for the Pentecost chapter, but Francis was far too ill to be present. He dictated a letter to be read at the

Body of St. Clare

chapter, which was chiefly a passionate appeal for increasing devotion to the blessed Sacrament, and he also dictated his Testament. This most precious document is his final confession of faith in his vocation, his final appeal to the fidelity of his followers. «Let not the Brothers say: «this is another Rule», because it is a reminder, an admonition and an exhortation and my last will and testament which I your lowly little brother Francis make for you my blessed brothers, so that we should in true Catholic fashion better observe the Rule which before the Lord we have promised to observe».

Towards the end of the summer a doctor friend from Arezzo came to see him. «Tell me Bembemgnate (another nickname) what do you think of this dropsy of mine?». At first «Bembemgnate» hedged; then seeing that Francis wanted the truth, told him that humanly speaking he could not live beyond late September or early October. Francis stretched up his arms: «Welcome Sister Death! To me she is the gate of life». He sent for the Brothers to sing the Canticle of the Creatures, and when they came to the end, Francis, radiant with joy, added a final verse:
«Praise be to Thee my Lord for our sister bodily death, From whom no living man can flee;
Woe to them who die in mortal sin
But blessed they who shall be found in Thy most holy will: To them the second death can do no harm».
Francis was in such a mood of exaltation that he continually wanted to hear song and singing; and the guards commented on it. Elias went to expostulate with him; «The men of this city think thee a saint, and believing that thou must shortly die when they hear these praises being sung by day and night they ask: «How is it that he thus openly rejoices, he who is about to die and should be thinking of his death?» Francis replied that thanks to a warning from Elias two years earlier he had indeed thought of his death every day, but now, «leave me Brother to rejoice in the Lord and in his praises and in my infirmities, for by the grace of the Holy Spirit working in me, I can well be merry in the Most High». He admitted when asked that his suffering was a martyrdom: he apologized to the brothers for all the trouble he gave them: «remember Our Lord will repay you for all you do for me». Rather late in the day he even apologized to his own body, «Brother Ass» for the harsh treatment he had received!
One day he seemed to be dying and the Brothers gathered round; Elias was on his left, Bernard on his right. He asked who was kneeling there, and crossing his hands, he said to Elias: «My son I bless thee in all things, through all things, and as the Most High has multiplied my brothers and sons in thy hands, so upon thee and in thee I bless

Grief of the Poor Clares

Moment of death

Tomb of St. Francis

Basilica of St. Francis

them all. May God the King of all bless thee in heaven and on earth. I bless thee as far as I can, and more than I can; and what I cannot do, may He do in thee Who can do all things». He called down a special blessing on Bernard: «Write», he said to Leo, «that as well as I am able, I wish and command that all Brothers in the whole Order shall honour Bernard as though he were myself, for he was the first who came to me and gave his goods to the poor». Francis rallied, and soon after this Elias obtained permission to take him to the Porziuncula. Certainly he would prefer to die in the sanctuary of Lady Poverty and not in a palace, even though it was not his own.

About half way down the hill his bearers paused at the hospital of the Crucigeri, and Francis asked them to turn his face to Assisi. He then prayed for, and blessed his city: «blessed be thou by God, holy city, because many servants of God will dwell in thee, and through thee many will be elected to the kingdom of eternal life. Peace be with thee».

What of Clare through these months? As long as Francis was in the Bishop's house, she must have hoped against hope that he might be able to be carried down to San Damiano, but when he was moved to the Porziuncula, that hope died. Through the last couple of years he had sent written words of encouragment and exhortation, and songs to San Damiano, and the bond between them had never been closer. Clare was very ill too at this time, but almost certainly she wrote to him, probably asking for advice as well as comfort, and Francis dictated a note: «I, little Brother Francis desire to follow the life and poverty of our most high Lord Jesus Christ, and of His most holy Mother, and to persevere therein until the end. And I beseech you, my ladies, and I counsel you always to live in this most holy life and poverty. And be very careful lest by the teaching or counsel of anyone, in any way, or at any time you should be drawn away from it».

He also sent Clare another message: «Go and tell Sister Clare to put aside all sorrow and sadness, for though she cannot now see me, yet before her death both she and her sisters shall see me, and have great comfort of me». In San Damiano every thought was at the Porziuncula, hidden in the woods a couple of miles away.

At that moment Francis remembers his other friend the Lady Giacoma di Settesoli; and he asked that a messenger should be sent to Rome telling her to come and to bring a grey habit, a cloth to cover his face, candles, and some almond cakes that he especially liked. But Giacoma had guessed what was happening, and before the messenger had even started she and her sons were knocking at the gate. «Now blessed be God», exclaimed Francis, «Who has sent us our Brother Giacoma. Open the gates and bring her in, for the rule concerning women is not for Brother Giacoma». Something would have been missing at Santa Maria degli Angeli in those days had Giacoma not been there to represent the immense outer circle of Francis' friends, his Third Order.

He also remembered his Porziuncula, and having had all the brothers called together he said: «See to it my Brothers that you never leave this place; if you are thrust out on one side, enter again by the other; for truly this place is holy, and the dwelling of God». He wished to be laid on the bare ground and to have his habit taken off, and he spoke again to the brothers: «I have done what was mine to do; may Christ teach you what is yours». Elias had a happy inspiration bringing Francis a habit, breeches and cap of sackcloth saying: «Know that this habit and breeches and cap are lent thee by me in holy obedience; and that thou mayest know that thou hast no right of property in them, I deprive thee of all power of giving them to anyone else». Francis' face beamed with joy at the thought that he had kept faith with Lady Poverty right up to the end. He blessed the Brothers again, and asked that the Passion according to Saint John should be read, and the Canticle sung, after which he still had strength to intone the 141st Psalm «I cried to the Lord with my voice». At the last verse, «bring my soul out of prison, that I may praise Thy name: the just wait for me until Thou reward me» «that most holy soul left the body and was received into the light of eternal life». «Francis poor and humble enters rich into Heaven».

It was the evening of October 3rd 1226: a multitude of larks were singing above the Porziuncula, and one Brother saw a brilliant orb of light borne by a little cloud ascending as it were across many waters swiftly into the sky.

The funeral procession was one of triumph with lights and hymns and waving olive branches. Francis was carried to San Damiano, and the Brothers lifted his body, and held it so that through the opened Communion grating Clare and the sisters could see and touch the wounds of the Stig-

St. Francis in glory

mata. Then they went on to the church of San Giorgio where Francis was temporarily buried.

Two years later he was canonized there by Cardinal Ugolino who had just become Pope Gregory IX. Pica's prophecy had been fulfilled, Francis' own prophecies too; and the Pope was justified when he said of his friend: «He shone in his days as the morning star in the midst of a cloud, or as the moon at its full. And as the sun when it shineth, so did he shine in the temple of God».

Within another two years his body in its travertine sarcophagus was translated to the resting place prepared for it deep beneath the high altar of the new church which the Pope, Brother Elias, and all Christendom wished to build and adorn in his honour. It is a pledge of the love and homage of mankind to the Little Poor Man who so loved God and his fellow-men.

To all who seek him, to the world to-day and always, Francis repeats his greeting, Pax et Bonum.

PRAYER FOR ALL

Lord make of me an instrument of Thy peace:
Where there is hatred, let me put love,
Where there is resentment let me put forgiveness,
Where there is discord let me put unity,
Where there is doubt let me put faith,
Where there is error let me put truth,
Where there is despair let me bring happiness,
Where there is sadness let me bring joy,
Where there is darkness let me bring light.

Master grant that I may desire rather:
To console than to be consoled.
To understand rather than to be understood.
To love rather than to be loved.

Because it is in giving that we receive;
In forgiving that we obtain forgiveness;
In dying that we rise to eternal life.

I N D E X